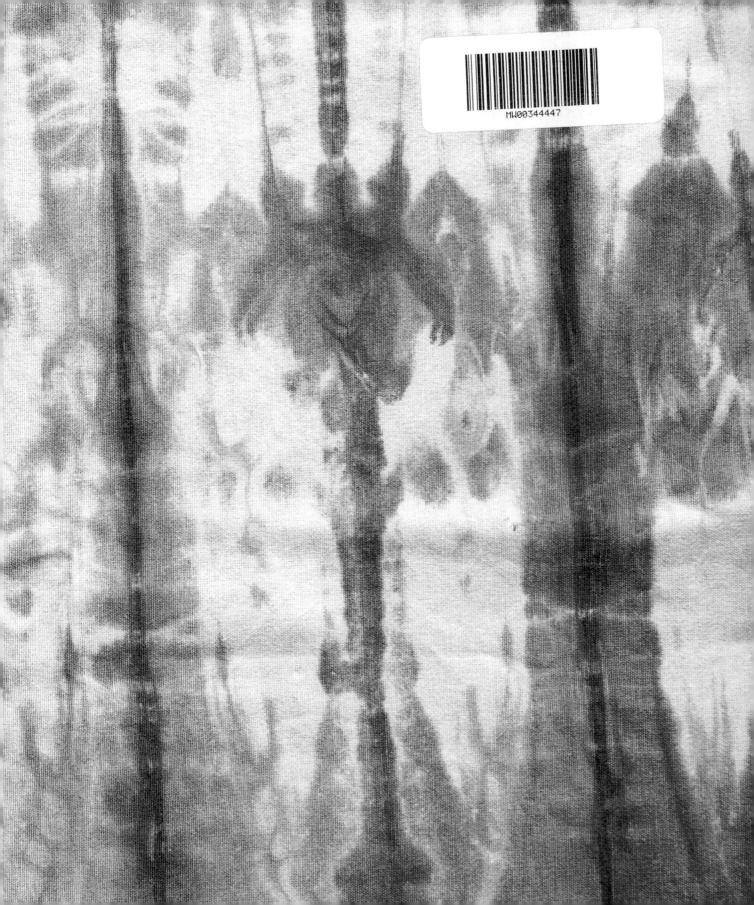

# HAND DYED

A Modern Guide to Dyeing in Brilliant Color for You and Your Home

ANNA JOYCE

PHOTOGRAPHY BY DANE TASHIMA

ABRAMS, NEW YORK

Editor: Meredith A. Clark
Designer: Brooke Reynolds for inchmark
Production Manager: Kathleen Gaffney

Library of Congress Control Number: 2018936227

ISBN: 978-1-4197-3428-1
eISBN: 978-1-68335-514-4

Printed and bound in China

10 9 8 7 6 5 4 3 2 1

Abrams books are available at special discounts when purchased in quantity for premiums and promotions as well as
fundraising or educational use. Special editions can also be
created to specification. For details, contact specialsales@
abramsbooks.com or the address below.

Abrams® is a registered trademark of Harry N. Abrams, Inc.

**ABRAMS** The Art of Books
195 Broadway, New York, NY 10007
abramsbooks.com

To my family—Victor, Angelina, and Iris—without whose love and support this book would not have been possible

# CONTENTS

# INTRODUCTION

**My love affair with dyeing happened suddenly and took me by surprise. I had just finished my first book, *Stamp Stencil Paint,* and was looking for something new to inspire me in the studio. I had been gifted an indigo dye kit, and one afternoon I decided to try it.**

I enjoyed the methodical process of setting up the dyebath and binding and tying the fabric. It was exciting to envision how the folds and shapes that I made would translate into patterns. When I pulled my test fabrics out of the indigo vat for the first time, I knew that there was no going back—I was hooked. This new way of working with dye seemed to combine everything that I loved about making art: the meditative process of working with fabric, the unexpected one-of-a-kind patterns, and the deep soulful colors the dyes can bring to a simple piece of cloth.

I was captivated. I began to dye everything I could get my hands on. It was inspiring to submerge a plain textile into the dyebath and then open it after an hour or two of soaking to reveal complex, often very surprising patterns and variations in color. It began to occur to me that dye was a way to record the ethereal and abstract patterns that water creates as it travels deep into the fibers of a textile.

My dye work began to expand into new materials and to grow in scale. At first, I used only the natural dyestuff indigo. The rich blue color was beautiful on every textile that I tried, and so many patterns looked lovely in the deep indigo blue that it seemed to be a foolproof way to explore designs and hone new ideas. I started to keep notes during my dye sessions and to take photos of folded bundles of cotton and silk before they went into the vat so I could remember how to reproduce any pleasing results.

As spring arrived in Portland that year, I found that I was craving even more color. Using dye, it was possible to blend white to pale pink to brilliant red or yellow with no hard lines or edges, just like the roses that grow with abandon here in Portland. Was it possible to achieve that magical transition of colors using dye and embed the beauty into fibers? Instead of indigo, I used fiber-reactive dyes to blend, mix, and explore, finding ease with the science and chemistry behind the colors I was playing with.

As I gained more knowledge and control over my results, I started to teach workshops at home and around the country. There is something very satisfying and almost miraculous about teaching someone to dye for the first time. It doesn't matter if you can't draw or you're not "crafty." Almost everyone can wrap rubber bands around cloth and fold fabric with the same level of confidence. I am amazed each class as I watch students delight in their results and leave with the courage to move forward and experiment.

Most of my classes start with shared observations about life, jobs, children, and partners in a truly meaningful way. Dyeing lends itself to working well together in groups, and the collaborative energy generated when making by hand with others naturally leads to laughter and solidarity. All the participants become involved: sharing baskets of supplies, tending to each other's work in the communal dye vat, and cheering each other on to try a new pattern. This feeling of community and of finding success with a new craft is something that brings me back to teaching and to working with dye again and again.

Intrigued by these observations, I started to investigate the history of hand dyeing, and I was not at all surprised to find that dyeing and textile production were often women's work. So the textiles we make and share when we dye by hand are part of a much richer tradition than just an afternoon craft project. The fabrics made by ancient textile makers—our ancestors—clothed and sheltered tribes, making it possible for them to hunt and survive the elements. Textiles, including clothing and other functional forms such as baskets, were responsible for helping create a sustainable community. To discover that this art form that I found so captivating was rooted in such a deep and essential historical context made me feel connected with other women and other artisans throughout time.

As I searched for more current information on dyeing by hand, I couldn't find books that offered a contemporary aesthetic or projects that reflected the styles that I was seeing in decor magazines and on design blogs. There are lots of informative books on tie-dye, but most of them focus on colors and patterns that you might associate with a bygone era and don't reflect the way we use hand-dyed goods today. There are also beautiful books on dyeing with natural dyes, but my small, 250-square-foot (76 × 76 m) studio was not large enough to house all the cooktops and supplies needed to effectively use these dyestuffs.

Eventually, I began to conceive of a book on dyeing by hand that was beautiful, inspiring, and, most important of all, contemporary. I wanted the projects to be simple enough that you could achieve great results even if this is your first time dyeing. Part 1 teaches you all about this easy approach to dyeing. Part 2 includes projects that inspire you to gather friends and family to create something beautiful together by hand, sharing conversation and laughter over a dye vat. *Hand Dyed* is about creating lovely projects that are inspired by ancient traditions but look at right at home in our modern lives.

Almost all the project patterns and colors in this book can be interchanged. The keys at the bottom of each project will let you know the kind of dye and fiber that was used. As long as the kind of dye and the kind of fiber are compatible,

colors and patterns can be easily mixed and matched (you'll learn more about the relationship between dye and fiber in the Dyeing Overview on page 12). Have fun folding new patterns and be sure to keep track of the results in a dye notebook, or by snapping photos on your smartphone.

I chose to concentrate on the use of fiber-reactive dyes and indigo for this book so the projects would be accessible to a large group of dyers. The development of synthetic dyes for hand dyers opened up a world of possibility for rich, playful colors, along with ease of use: The advent of fiber-reactive, cold-water dyes meant that heat was no longer needed to set dyes and offered the flexibility to dye a wide array of fibers. If you have concerns about the ecological footprint of using synthetic dyes, note that these dyes are not intrinsically bad for the environment just because they are not "natural." Fiber-reactive dye and other synthetics, like the ones used in this book, are no less environmentally friendly than natural dyes, so you can feel good about using them, knowing they are not any more harmful to the environment.

Most well-stocked craft stores should have a good selection of fiber-reactive dyes, soda ash, and materials such as rubber bands, twine, and clamps for making resists. If you do not live near a well-stocked craft store, all the materials used in *Hand Dyed* can be easily purchased online. See the full list of resources on page 158.

Fiber-reactive dyes are easy to find and simple to use, and provide an unlimited variety of exciting colors and techniques. If you're intrigued by the ageless allure of indigo, you'll find information about how to work with it, as well. While the dyes that are used in *Hand Dyed* are mostly new, the techniques and traditions that inspire the patterns for each project are ancient and steeped in history. I hope you will gather friends and family and explore the colorful, creative, and ageless art of dyeing by hand.

# Dyeing Overview

The two primary dye processes used in *Hand Dyed*—fiber-reactive dyeing and indigo dyeing—impart color to a plain textile through chemical reactions, though each process works in a different way. The outcome is also dependent on the interplay between the type of dye and the type of fiber to which it is applied, both of which are explored in this section. I also share a glossary of dye terminology, so you are familiar with the terms as you read through the sections in part 1. And I offer a window into the different ways dyes can be applied in the projects in part 2.

## TYPES OF DYE

*To begin your exploration of color on fiber, first familiarize yourself with the types of dyes you will be using for the projects in this book.*

### FIBER-REACTIVE DYE

Fiber-reactive dye is my favorite type of dye to work with—it is easy to use and provides brilliant, permanent color in cold water, making it perfect for backyard projects and spontaneous dye sessions. This type of dye creates its vivid colors on cellulose and protein fibers (see pages 13–16), such as cotton, linen, silk, or wool, by forming a chemical bond to the fiber's molecules, permanently changing the color of the fiber at a molecular level. This means that the color actually becomes part of the fiber, creating a color-fast change that will not wash out. Fiber-reactive dyes are used throughout this book on a variety of textiles. I love the vibrant colors that are possible with fiber-reactive dyes, and they are great for beginners because they are easy to use, inexpensive, and extremely versatile.

### A BASIC RULE

Here is a basic rule for dyeing with fiber-reactive dyes—darker colors require more dye per pound (kg) of fabric, while pastel colors will need less. When working with fiber-reactive dyes, you should always test your materials for the most accurate results. This is especially important when using fiber-reactive dye on protein fibers such as silk or wool, as the dye can shift and change colors depending on the substrate (see page 19). (Although acid dyes, explained in the following section, are generally used with protein fibers, fiber-reactive dyes can also be used successfully on these textiles, as you'll see in the Silk Ribbons project on page 71.)

Fiber-reactive dyes will stay active for a few days or even weeks when mixed with pure water, gradually losing strength over time. But when fiber-reactive dyes are combined with any amount of soda ash in the dyebath, as is occasionally required, they will lose all strength and become inactive after only a few hours. Learn more about soda ash in Dyeing Basics (see page 27); it plays an important role in the dyeing process.

## ACID DYE

Acid dyes are used to achieve brilliant colors on protein fibers (see page 16) such as wool, silk, cashmere, and angora. These dyes have an acidic base, such as gentle vinegar or citric acid, and heat is used as a mordant (see page 18) for protein fibers to create super-saturated colors. Since acid dyes require heat to activate, plan ahead to have access to boiling water or a cooktop when working with them.

## INDIGO

Indigo dye, derived from the leaves of the indigo plant, is one of the oldest methods used to dye and print textiles. It is one of the only blue dyes found in nature. Indigo-bearing plants grow all over the world, and indigo's unique, deep blue is a part of natural dye traditions in many cultures.

Indigo is an unusual dye in that it needs no mordant (see page 18) and undergoes a chemical reaction with oxygen to create the rich, dark blue that takes its name. Indigo first must undergo a reduction process (see page 30) in order to become active, because it does not naturally dissolve in water. For the projects in this book, I used indigo that has been pre-reduced via a chemical process so that the dye will dissolve in water, which greatly simplifies dyeing with indigo. In its liquid state, the indigo dye turns an electric yellow-green color, and when fibers are removed from the vat (the traditional name for the indigo dyebath), they will retain that yellow-green color until they interact with the oxygen in the air and begin to turn the distinctive blue color; this is called oxidizing (see page 18). One indigo vat is capable of creating an incredible range from sky blue to a rich navy, based on the number of times an item is dipped into the vat and allowed to oxidize. The more times a fiber is dipped into the indigo and allowed to oxidize, the darker the blue will become. Short, frequent dips in the indigo, followed by oxidation, result in the deepest blue hues.

## WATERCOLOR AS A DYE?

Indeed! You can use concentrated watercolor to achieve lovely transparent colors on paper. These paints are primarily designed for fine or graphic arts, but the transparent paints blend and work beautifully in the Orizomegami Wrapping Paper project on page 59, as well. The types used in that project come in glass bottles with a handy eye-dropper, so they are simple to use.

## TYPES OF FIBER

*Did you know that wool and cotton are composed of very different types of fibers? Wool, cashmere, silk, and angora are called protein fibers, because they are created from the fur of animals or the filament from a silkworm. Cotton, linen, bamboo, rayon, and hemp are cellulose fibers, because they are derived from plants. Because the chemical structures of these two fibers are so different, they generally require different types of dyes to achieve the greatest range of color. I have included specific references to the type of fiber and the type of dye used in the projects, so you can explore dyeing any kind of fiber with confidence.*

## CELLULOSE FIBERS

You can use fiber-reactive dyes or indigo with these fabrics with equal success. Because they are plant-based, you can also interchange them to a certain degree when you are dyeing—the three fibers that are totally interchangeable in these projects are cotton, linen, and rayon. These cellulose fibers each have their own unique qualities and will take dye with subtle variations in color and texture, but in any project that calls for cotton, you can exchange the fiber for rayon or linen with no change to the instructions. Feel free to experiment!

## Cellulose Fibers

Cellulose (or plant-based) fibers take dye beautifully in many different forms including yardage, ribbon, lace, and yarn.

Protein Fibers

Synthetic Fibers

Protein fibers, derived from animals or the silkworm, generally require an acid-based dye and hot water for best results.

Synthetic (man-made) fibers are best dyed with products formulated especially for their unique characteristics.

## THE BURN TEST

If you are unable to identify a fiber by the way it looks or feels, you can conduct what is called a "burn test." During this test, fibers will burn, melt, smell, and produce ash in a characteristic way that helps you identify an unknown fiber.

First, make sure you do this safely! Be very careful when testing unknown fibers, because synthetic fibers often melt and produce hazardous fumes. Always work in a well-ventilated area (or outside on a calm day), and have a fire extinguisher and/or bucket of water at hand. You will need tweezers or tongs to hold the fabric and a fireproof metal or glass container to work over. A large ashtray is perfect. It's best to use a regular disposable lighter, as they do not produce the heavy smell that matches or refillable lighters do. Start with a small scrap of the fabric in question, perhaps 1 by 2" (2.5 by 5 cm) or so.

Touch the flame to the fabric, holding it over the container. Observe as it burns and check the residue:

• Cellulose fibers ignite and burn quickly, with white smoke and a glowing ember after the fire is extinguished. The smoke will smell like burning paper or leaves, leaving behind a soft, white ash.

• Protein fibers burn slowly and will shrink away from the flame. They will often smell of burning hair and their residue is dark and brittle.

• Synthetic fibers burn quickly and can continue to burn after the flame is removed, sometimes melting and dripping into beads of plastic. There will be black smoke and a chemical smell of burning plastic.

## PROTEIN FIBERS

Protein fibers are derived from animals or insects, so wool, silk, cashmere, and angora are all protein fibers. Acid dyes and indigo dye both work well with protein fibers. As explained earlier, some protein fibers can also be dyed with fiber-reactive dyes, but be sure to read any special instructions and test your materials carefully, as the fiber-reactive dye will respond differently than it does with cellulose fibers.

A special note: Protein fibers are often more delicate than cellulose fibers. Take care to use lukewarm water and gentle agitation when washing to keep from shocking or felting the fibers; shocking makes silk brittle, while felting locks wool fibers into a mat.

## SYNTHETIC FIBERS

Synthetic fibers are man-made materials such as polyester, spandex, acrylic, and nylon. There are dyes made specifically for synthetic fibers such as iDye Poly, which uses heat and a special dye blend to create brilliant colors on otherwise hard-to-dye synthetic fibers.

## FIBER BLENDS

When you have two fibers that are blended together, such as cotton and spandex or silk and wool, it is important to identify which fiber is present in the highest percentage. This will help you choose the appropriate dye. Items that are mostly cotton work well with fiber-reactive dyes, while a largely synthetic item might need to be dyed with a specialty dye (see above). You will want to choose the dye that is compatible with the fiber that is dominant in the blend. Generally, you can find this information on the fabric bolt (if you're purchasing yardage) or the item label (if you're dyeing a commercial piece such as a scarf or tablecloth). If you're not sure about the content of the fiber you're dyeing, see the sidebar at left.

# TYPES OF DYE APPLICATION

*Just as there are different types of dye, there are different ways to apply it to a textile. All the methods detailed below are demonstrated in the projects in part 2.*

### TUB DYEING

Tub dyeing (also called vat dyeing or garment dyeing) is aptly named: This is simply dyeing items in a tub or a bucket filled with a large quantity of water and dissolved dye **(A)**. Fiber-reactive dyes work very well for tub dyeing. You will find many examples of tub dyeing here, including the Tropical Green Kaftan (see page 95) and the Storm Clouds Duvet Set (see page 111).

### DIRECT APPLICATION DYEING

Direct application dyeing is aptly named, as well: a dye mixture is applied directly onto the fiber **(B)**. The results from direct application dyeing are often very saturated and give the dyer a lot of control when mixing and applying colors onto a fiber. The Confetti Quilt (see page 129) is an example of direct application with dry dye.

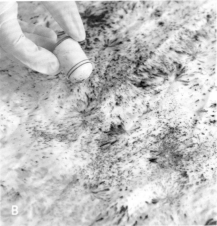

### ICE DYE

Ice dyeing is a fun and surprising way to dye, as it yields otherworldly patterns **(C)**. In this variation of the direct application technique, pre-soaked fibers are covered in a pile of ice and then powdered dye is applied directly on top. As the ice melts, the dye dissolves and soaks through the fiber. When the powdered dye particles hit the ice, they begin to dissolve and expand, breaking into little explosions of often unexpected color. A color such as eggplant purple can leave behind yellows, greens, pinks, and deep purples when ice dyeing. When you are using this technique, the color you choose must be compatible with cold water. Black, for instance, needs heat to activate and will not work for ice dyeing. See the Northern Lights Scarf on page 97 for a lovely example of this technique.

You can get an idea of what colors the dye will "break" into when ice dyeing by testing it in a clean container of water: Add a tiny dash of dye onto the surface of the water; when the dye hits the water, it will separate as the molecules begin to dissolve. To test several colors at a time, you can also sprinkle tiny amounts of dye onto single ice cubes set atop a scrap of fabric. You will probably be surprised by the results!

# DYE TERMINOLOGY

*As you read through* Hand Dyed, *you will see many of the terms that are defined below, and they may be mentioned in a variety of contexts. Here is a short introduction to the concepts used throughout. As you will discover, dyeing is actually working with a chemical reaction as the medium. I find this process to be endlessly fascinating and inspiring!*

**Dye, dyestuff** A dye (or dyestuff) is a natural or synthetic substance that is capable of changing the color of the substrate (see below) to which it is applied. Generally, dye is mixed with water, which is then referred to as the dyebath (see below). Unlike paint, where a colored pigment is suspended in a medium such as water or oil and then applied to the surface of a substrate, dye actually forms a chemical bond with the material that it touches and changes its color on a molecular level. After a substrate has been dyed, the color is permanent.

Because the colors result from a chemical reaction to the specific fiber the dye encounters, there can be a lot of variation in the hues that result when you use the same color dye on a different fiber. For instance, even though cotton and linen are both cellulose fibers (see page 13), they can often have slight variations in the finished results even when dyed the same color.

**Dyebath** This is the common term for the dye solution used in the dyeing process.

**Curing** Curing describes the process of allowing an item to rest after having been dyed with fiber-reactive dye; dyed goods or items should sit for at least twelve and ideally up to twenty-four hours before undoing any resists (see below) or rinsing and washing. Curing lets the colors deepen and develop and helps the patterns remain crisp and defined. The chemical bonds that occur in the dyeing process continue in a fiber for up to twenty-four hours, so rinsing an item too soon leads to pale, washed-out colors and fuzzy patterns. To see an example of how curing affects the final results, see page 28.

**Flower** This term describes the bubbles and foam that rise to the top of an indigo vat. The flower should be gently skimmed off the top before dyeing.

**Mordant** A mordant is a fixative that helps the dye bond permanently with the fiber that it is being applied to. The mordant that we will be using most commonly is soda ash. You will learn more about the use of soda ash in Dyeing Basics (see page 27).

**Oxidize, oxidization** Oxidization is the reaction that a fiber undergoes when it comes in contact with oxygen after being saturated with indigo dye. Fibers go from an electric yellow-green to deep indigo blue when they are exposed to the oxygen in air.

**Reduced, pre-reduced** In its natural state, indigo is insoluble in water and will not dye unless it is reduced—meaning the oxygen is removed from the dyebath through a time-consuming reduction process. The indigo used in *Hand Dyed* is pre-reduced, however, as it has been treated chemically so that it will dissolve in water.

**Resist** A resist is anything that keeps the dye from making contact with the fiber. When the resists are removed, the undyed areas form a pattern. Rubber bands, string, twine, and clamps are used as resists to make many of the patterns you will see here, although there are other kinds of resists that can be applied to keep the dye from penetrating the surface of the substrate. For example, wax, rice paste, and even water-based craft glue can be used to form a pattern. These kinds of resists can be applied using brushes, stencils, and specialty applicators. There is more detailed information about the various kinds of resists used in this book on page 22.

**Reverse dyeing** Most of the projects in this book are additive in nature, meaning color is being added to a fiber, but you can also create beautiful patterns and achieve stunning results by taking color away as well. These "reverse" patterns can be created with bleach pastes and heat-activated color removers; these products can also be used to lighten or remove the color from an existing textile. See the Points of Light Pillows project on page 123 for an interpretation of this technique.

**Scour, scouring** Scouring is the term used to describe the thorough cleaning a fiber must undergo before it is hand dyed. Most fibers have dirt, oil, and starches on them that make it impossible for the dye to penetrate evenly. Read more about scouring on page 26.

**Slurry** A slurry is a concentrated mixture of dry dye dissolved into a small amount of water; a typical slurry may be mixed with ½ cup (120 ml) of water and the amount of dye listed in a given project. Slurries are then added to a larger container of water to create the dyebath. Making a slurry with your dye and water helps to eliminate spotting and uneven dyeing caused by undissolved powdered dye in the dyebath.

**Substrate** A substrate is a surface or material on which something will be applied—for the purposes of this book, that substrate will most often be a textile or woven fiber, sometimes in the form of a finished garment or home decor item.

**Vat** Traditionally, the vessel that contains indigo dye is referred to as a vat. Here I use a 5-gallon (19 L) plastic container for the vat; a container with high sides and a tightly fitting lid is ideal. See more information about dyeing with indigo on page 30.

# Gathering Tools and Materials

Dyeing by hand has a reputation for being messy, but with a few common supplies and a little bit of preparation, the dye process can be relatively clean. Before you begin a dyeing project, you will need to gather a variety of supplies, many of which you may already have on hand. For specialty materials, consult Resources on page 158 for a list of suppliers.

## BASIC DYER'S KIT

*Here are the items I suggest having on hand for your Dyer's Kit. Everything that you need can fit into a large storage container, making it easy to use when you are inspired to dye, but simple to store when the project is over. When you're ready to dive into the projects, the Dyer's Kit listing will also specify whether you need multiples or a specific size of a particular item for a project—such as three dozen clothespins or four shallow containers, for example.*

Some additional considerations to keep in mind before you begin: First, you need a flat surface to work on; a table or floor can be used for dyeing if it is covered properly with a plastic tarp or painter's drop cloth. Second, it is best to have ready access to water! When I started my dye practice I did not have a sink in my studio. I would have to fill buckets in the utility sink, carry them down two flights of stairs, and store the water under my studio table. Many dye projects can be done with very little water, but having access to a sink or a hose is ideal.

## SAFETY GEAR

I begin with the important things: Be sure to wear a respirator mask and rubber gloves while you work with powdered dye. It is best to work in a well-ventilated space and wear a face mask to protect your lungs from airborne particulates when mixing dyes and chemicals.

Rubber gloves are essential to keep your hands from being stained and to keep your skin safe from chemical irritants. I like to wear a pair of heavy-duty rubber gloves when working on a particularly messy job. I also keep a box of thin, disposable rubber or latex gloves handy in the studio to wear for tasks that involve finer motor skills, such as untying goods after they are removed from a dyebath.

## MEASURING AND MIXING TOOLS

I use standard measuring cups and spoons to measure my dye and chemicals. You should have a separate set for dyeing so that you never use the same utensils for dye as you do for food preparation. I also have a small set of plastic funnels for adding dye and chemicals to small-mouth containers without making a mess.

For mixing, I use inexpensive wooden spoons or dowels. The wood takes on a beautiful patina of dye colors and is easy to clean, pretty to have around, and useful for mixing custom colors (see pages 44–51). Do make sure you keep one "clean spoon" or stir stick so you do not transfer trace dyes onto clean items that you're removing from a water or soda ash bath, and only use indigo sticks in indigo. (One speck of unwanted dye can ruin a project! Try to make sure that your workspace stays clean by wiping up any spills right away, and try to not let powdered dye become airborne.) Long metal tongs are good for turning your pieces when they are soaking in a dyebath or for easily retrieving small pieces from the bottom of a vat.

**Many of the items you need to assemble for your Dyer's Kit may be in your home already. Any kitchen items used for dyeing should not be used again for food preparation—keep them in the dye studio.**

## PLASTIC AND GLASS CONTAINERS

The containers that I use the most in my studio are 1-, 3-, and 5-gallon (3.8, 11.4, and 19 L) plastic containers and small glass canning jars (pint [500 ml] and quart [.9 L] size). Traditional straight-sided buckets are wonderful and can be found at almost any hardware store; however, I also like to use wider, shallower plastic containers for large bulky items that may be too wide to fit into a round bucket, such as the Storm Clouds Duvet Set on page 111. The plastic buckets and containers can usually be found in the paint department of the hardware store. You can use these containers for everything: mixing custom colors and chemicals, presoaking your items, immersing your projects in a dyebath, storing projects while they cure (see page 18), rinsing, and transporting finished projects to the laundry. It is a good idea to keep several buckets on hand. I also like to keep a variety of smaller yogurt and takeout containers in my studio so I always have a clean container on hand when I need it.

A good mix for a Dyer's Kit would be two 5-gallon (19 L) buckets, one 5-gallon (19 L) wide plastic storage container, two to four 1-gallon (3.8 L) plastic containers, and three to six 1-quart (.9 L) containers for smaller projects.

## RAGS AND PAPER TOWELS

I keep a basket of rags handy when I am dyeing, because they are invaluable for cleaning up spills and splashes—and the colors that build up over time make them a work of art themselves! Having a roll of paper towels is always a good idea, too, but I prefer thirsty, reusable cotton rags. Make sure to machine-wash your used rags often—stray dye from a messy project can easily transfer.

## NEWSPRINT AND CANVAS DROP CLOTHS

A stash of inexpensive newsprint paper is invaluable; 20 × 30" (50 × 75 cm) sheets are a nice large size. You can use a sheet to soak up extra dye under a project, to protect your work surface from powdered dye, and as a clean surface for folding and working with clean textiles. It is also a good idea to have a large canvas drop cloth in your Dyer's Kit. A good drop cloth will protect the ground under your dye area indoors and out. Look for canvas drop cloths with a plastic backing—these will offer the best protection from spills.

## PLASTIC BAGS

Plastic bags are used for storing dye projects that need to cure overnight while staying wet. I keep a roll of kitchen garbage bags handy for curing my projects and transporting them to the laundry. You can also save recycled grocery bags, plastic wrap, or anything else that will keep your textiles damp for twenty-four hours during the curing process.

## RESISTS

As you will learn, there is a multitude of items that can be used for resists, but common items such as rubber bands, twine, clamps, and clothespins are the tools that I use most. I like to have a variety of rubber bands in different thicknesses and sizes. The twine or thread that you use to bind your projects can be fun to play with—thin cotton twine is useful and good for most projects, but you may want to experiment with dental floss, fishing line, zip ties, or anything else that will bind your fabric and resist the dye.

I also use a lot of C-clamps and spring clamps, which you can find at almost any hardware store—probably your local grocery, as well. Having a variety of clamps that range in size is invaluable! Larger clamps allow you to bind bulky items, and smaller clamps create a good amount of pressure to ensure crisp results on smaller items. I also like to make patterns using clamps or clothespins as a design element; for the Tropical Green Kaftan on page 95, a simple accordion fold held tight with clothespins resisted the dye and yielded a beautiful result.

## CLOTHESLINE OR DRYING RACK

Dyeing outside on a sunny day with a clothesline is ideal—and it's a great way to be inspired by nature—but when that is not possible, it is good to have a drying rack handy. I like to use a collapsible drying rack in my studio when I am working in cold weather or when I am teaching someplace where I cannot hang a clothesline. Inexpensive racks are very easy to come by.

## TEST MATERIAL

Testing your dye is essential for the best results. Many powdered dyes are not at all the color they appear to be when they are dry. For instance, one of my favorite sea-green colors looks like a soft gray in the container. There is no way to tell the tone of a new color without mixing up a small amount and testing it on a swatch of fabric. The final color of the dye will depend on a wide range of factors—how long the textile is allowed to soak in the dye, the concentration of the dye solution, and the type of fiber that you are dyeing. I have taken most of the guesswork out of the projects in this book by figuring out the color formulas for you, but here is how to test dyes on your own: Simply soak a strip of cotton or linen in the test bath for about twenty minutes. This will give you a good idea of the overall color and tone of the dye or custom blend. I like to make a small dye bath in a glass jelly jar (¼ teaspoon of dye to 1 cup [240 ml] of water is a good ratio for a test bath) and submerge one end of the test strip in the solution. This allows the dye solution to wick up into the fabric and gives you a nice range of tones and undertones in the color.

## NOTEBOOK

I will often be inspired to blend a custom color or try a new folding technique, and if I do not keep track of the recipe it is often difficult—if not impossible—to re-create later. Therefore, I keep a journal when I am dyeing, taking good notes of custom color blends and experimental binding and folding techniques. I keep track of dye recipes, ideas, and results, and I even glue color swatches into my dye journal. It makes reproducing colors and patterns much easier, and it is a great place to record inspiration.

## PROFESSIONAL TEXTILE DETERGENT

Professional textile detergents (PTDs) are specially formulated for dye artists. They are used both for scouring

One of the most important tools for successful dyeing is a notebook! Keep track of your experiments and formulas so you can replicate your results. I keep swatches in my notebook for quick reference.

(before dyeing) and for rinsing (after dyeing) and are a must for your Dyer's Kit. There are several good products on the market, including Synthrapol and Dharma Professional Textile Detergent.

Prewashing with a PTD removes the invisible dirt, oil, starches, and impurities that can keep the dye from bonding with your fiber and cause uneven dyeing. As a final wash after dyeing, this neutral pH detergent also removes the excess dye molecules that have not been chemically bonded to the fabric so they do not make your project dull or muddy. This step will also keep your projects from bleeding and transferring dye to other items. As a general rule, use ¼ cup (2 liquid ounces/60 ml) of PTD per full washing machine load for cellulose fibers (cotton, rayon, linen, etc.) and 2 table-spoons (1 liquid ounce/30 ml) for silks. If hand-washing, a capful or so is all that is needed. Consult the detergent man-ufacturer's directions for more specific information.

## MISCELLANEOUS SUPPLIES

There are a few common household items you'll want to add to your Dyer's Kit, including fabric and paper scissors, a mea-suring tape or ruler, masking tape, and a permanent marker. I use the tape and marker often to label test swatches and keep track of custom blends in the studio, for example. A kitchen timer is also helpful, especially when working with indigo. You'll need an iron and ironing board as well.

### SPECIAL AGENTS AND ADDITIVES

There are a few additional supplies that you will need to have on hand for a dyeing session, but the amounts you need will vary from project to proj-ect. Each set of instructions will tell you how much soda ash, dyer's salt, citric acid, or vinegar you may need. Each has a different purpose: Soda ash is a mordant for fiber-reactive dyeing (see page 12), while dyer's salt helps push the dye molecules out of the water and into the fabric, making for darker, more intense colors. (Regular noniodized salt will also work for this purpose.) Citric acid or vinegar is needed for dyeing protein fibers with acid dyes (see page 13), as it lowers the pH of the dyebath to improve the dye's chemical bond with the fiber.

## DYER'S KIT AT A GLANCE

*Here's a quick reference guide to the items I suggest having in your Dyer's Kit.*

- Safety gear
- Measuring and mixing tools
- Plastic and glass containers
- Rags and paper towels
- Newsprint and/or drop cloth
- Plastic bags
- Resists (clamps, twine, rubber bands, etc.)
- Drying rack or clothesline
- Test material
- Soda ash
- Dyer's salt
- Citric acid or vinegar
- Professional textile detergent
- Fabric and paper scissors
- Measuring tape or ruler
- Masking tape
- Permanent marker
- Timer
- Iron and ironing board
- Notebook

# Dyeing Basics

In this section, I share the basic step-by-step processes for each type of dye used for the projects in this book. The project instructions themselves give specific directions about how I created each pattern and the amounts of dye (or dyes) that I used. For the overview, I begin with fiber-reactive dye, and then move to the different, but no less magical, indigo process.

## DYEING WITH FIBER-REACTIVE DYES

*As explained earlier, when fiber-reactive dye is dissolved in water and makes contact with a fiber, a chemical reaction takes place that changes the fiber on a molecular level, resulting in a permanent change in the fiber's color. The longer the chemical reaction is allowed to take place, the darker and more vibrant the colors will be. Even though the dye colors and substrates may vary, dyeing with fiber-reactive dye involves the same basic processes. And to make sure that the chemical reaction can take place properly, the fiber must be prepared first.*

## STEP-BY-STEP FOR FIBER-REACTIVE DYES

### 1. Scour the Textile

Scouring is the term used to describe the thorough cleaning a textile must undergo before it is hand dyed. Most fibers have dirt, oil, and starches on them that make it impossible for the dye to penetrate the surface evenly, whether this is a length of yardage or a commercially produced item you plan to dye. Scouring most of the items used for these projects is easy: simply machine- or hand-wash with hot water and a professional textile detergent (PTD; see page 23) and hang or machine-dry **(A)**. For machine-washing, use ¼ cup (2 liquid ounces/60 ml) textile detergent for cellulose fibers and 2 tablespoons (1 liquid ounce/30 ml) for protein fibers; for hand-washing, a capful or two is usually sufficient. Consult the label on the specific product you are using for additional details; for example, you may need to use cool or warm (not hot) water for protein fibers.

If the textile or item is heavily starched (stiff), such as the twill tape used in the Ribbon Top Baskets on page 139, it will require special attention: Simmer with small amount of soda ash and detergent to effectively scour it. If all the starches and additives in the textile are not properly removed, the dye will not be able to penetrate the textile.

## 2. Add the Resist

If you are making any of the resist-dyed projects in the book, you will add some type of resist at this stage **(B)**. These techniques are outlined in Making Patterns (see page 34), and specific directions are found in each set of project instructions.

## 3. Mordant the Fiber

The next step is to mordant the fibers. Depending on the fiber content of your goods, the mordant may change, but most commonly I use soda ash. Soaking a fiber in soda ash raises the pH level and prepares it to accept fiber-reactive dye and form that permanent color bond with the molecules of the textile.

To make an all-purpose soak, the ratio is 1 cup (227 g) of soda ash per 1 gallon (3.8 L) of water. (Note that many of the larger projects need to soak in a 5-gallon [19 L] batch of soda ash so they can be completely submerged. Make as little or as much as you need following this recipe, be sure your textiles are totally covered in the solution during the mordanting step.) Pour the soda ash in a container of warm water and stir with a long spoon or stick until it is dissolved **(C)**.

The soda ash mixture can be used for several projects or until all the liquid has been absorbed. Start over with new water and fresh soda ash if the bucket becomes contaminated with dye (spills do happen!) or when the water gets especially dirty. The majority of the projects in *Hand Dyed* were soaked in a soda ash solution for at least twenty minutes before being dyed. Consult the specific project to see if the fibers need to folded, bound, or tied before being soaked in the soda ash solution.

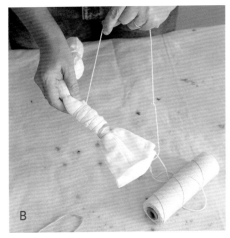

### ALL-IN-ONE DYEBATH

Occasionally, it makes more sense to add the soda ash directly to the dyebath, so you mordant and dye the fibers at the same time. I like to use this "all in one" method for very large and bulky items, or for a dip-dyeing project such as the Festive Cotton Buntings on page 67, because it helps me control the amount of liquid that soaks into the fiber. If you are dyeing a solid color, it can also save you a step. Remember, however, that the dye will begin to lose its potency as soon as the soda ash is added, so plan ahead and have everything ready to dye as soon as you prepare an all-in-one dyebath.

### 4. Mix the Dye

Many of the projects require that you measure and mix the dye before you apply it to your project. For the purposes of this beginner's hand-book, the amounts of dye used for most of the projects are measured with simple kitchen measuring spoons, and all the projects can be successfully created using these simple tools (D). If you move on to more advanced fiber-reactive dyeing beyond the scope of this book, note that it's best to use a digital kitchen scale to weigh both dyestuffs and the goods being dyed to achieve the greatest accuracy in reproducing color.

In several projects, a slurry (see page 19) of dye is added to the water in the tub or container (E). A slurry usually consists of about ½ cup (120 ml) of water, along with the amount of dye recommended for the project; some project instructions may offer specific ratios for the slurry.

### 5. Apply the Dye

Dye is applied to fiber in a variety of ways in this book (see page 17), giving you a number of options to choose from. Most often powdered dye is mixed into a large container of water to create a dyebath, in which the fiber is then immersed (tub or vat dyeing, seen in F). But dye can also be applied to the textile as a dry powder (direct application, as shown in the Confetti Quilt on page 129). This technique also has a variation in which dry dye is applied to ice placed on top of the textile (ice dyeing, seen in the Sunrise Blouse on page 83). Dye can also be stamped onto a project, as shown in the Stamped Table Linens on page 107. The application of the dye depends on the desired results, so look to the project instructions for guidance in each individual case.

### 6. Cure the Fiber

Many of the fiber-reactive dye projects need to be cured in a plastic bag for up to twenty-four hours. This allows all the chemical bonds that happen between the dye and the fiber to strengthen; this also lessens the amount of dye that needs to be removed during washing (see opposite). Don't be tempted to hurry through this important part of the process, because it allows the dye to penetrate deep into the fibers of the textile, ensuring the most saturated colors and crispest patterns. Here is a good visual comparison: These two pieces of linen were each tied and dyed in the same way. The first was rinsed out right after dyeing (G) and the second was allowed to cure for twenty-four hours in a plastic bag (H).

## 7. Rinse and Wash

After dyeing, fibers should first be rinsed in cold water to stop the chemical reactions taking place between the dye and the fiber; this also removes excess dye from the project. If possible, rinse the fibers until the water runs clear and no excess dye remains. Then hand- or machine-wash the item in hot water with a professional textile detergent (following the manufacturer's directions to remove any remaining dye from the fibers; see page 23).

That said, note that not all fibers like to be washed in very cold or very hot water. Protein fibers such as silk and wool need to be handled more delicately than cellulose fibers such as cotton or rayon. Special washing instructions are listed for each project, but a good rule of thumb is to hand-wash silk in room-temperature water. When silk is exposed to extreme hot or cold it can "shock" the fibers, causing them to lose their soft texture. After washing, it's generally recommended to let dyed items air-dry (I), though many can be successfully machine-dried.

## 8. Dispose of the Dyebath

Fiber-reactive dyes can be safely disposed of by pouring them down the drain. As an alternative, look for a place to pour them outside, away from plants and animals. When disposing of your dyebath in a sink, make sure there are no eating or cooking utensils in the sink, and rinse any excess dye down the drain. Clean the sink with a mild cleanser.

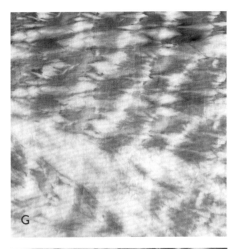

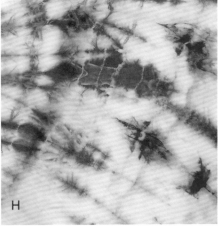

# DYEING WITH INDIGO

*Indigo blue is one of the most recognizable colors in the world, used for dyeing textiles in many different cultures throughout the ages because indigo-bearing plants grow in a variety of different climates. Here is how to begin your exploration of this ancient natural dyestuff.*

## SETTING UP AN INDIGO VAT

There are several very good indigo kits on the market that make setting up an indigo vat completely foolproof, because all the chemical components are pre-measured for success. See Resources on page 158 for ordering information.

However, if you find you love the indigo dyeing process like I do and you plan to dye in bulk, you will likely want to make your own indigo vats to save time and money. Unlike the fiber-reactive dye recipes, you must have a basic kitchen scale to measure the indigo dye ingredients needed to make a vat. See Resources on page 158 for information on purchasing your own tools and supplies for an indigo vat.

You will see that the recipe below uses pre-reduced indigo. In its natural, raw state, indigo is not water soluble, so it takes considerable effort, knowledge, and time to create an active indigo bath. As an easy alternative, pre-reduced indigo crystals have been treated to dissolve in water and will transform into a thriving vat with the simple addition of soda ash and a reducing agent, such as sodium hydrosulfite, which removes the oxygen from the vat. (You can also use sodium hydrosulfite as a color remover in place of bleach in reverse-dyeing projects, where you are removing color instead of adding it.) An indigo vat made with pre-reduced indigo crystals gives the same unique results as regular indigo, sets up in about fifteen minutes, and has a very low environmental footprint.

## CARING FOR AN INDIGO VAT

An indigo vat can live a long, happy life if it is properly tended. Here are some tips for success:

• Always replace and stir the flower (see page 18) back into the vat after dyeing.

• Use a container with a tight-fitting lid to keep excess oxygen from entering the vat.

• Always check your vat before dyeing to make sure that the indigo vat is still chemically active. It should be a vibrant yellow-green under the dark blue flower on the top of the vat.

• If possible, store your indigo vat in a warm room, which will help it last longer.

If you have used the indigo vat for a project or two or it has been left unattended for a few days, you may need to test the strength of the vat to see if the dye is still active. Use a swatch of test fabric to check the vat and recalibrate the chemicals as needed (see the sidebar on page 32).

### NOTE

Each time oxygen is introduced to the vat it changes the pH balance of the vat, making it less potent. Adding as little oxygen as possible to the vat while stirring keeps the chemicals in the vat strong and ready to bond with the fibers you are dyeing.

## BASIC INDIGO VAT RECIPE

This recipe is calibrated for 4 gallons (15.4 L) of liquid in a 5-gallon (19 L) container. This vat size is appropriate for all the indigo projects in part 2.

## Supplies

5-gallon (19 L) container with a tightly fitting lid

Small container, for storing the flower

Rubber gloves

Dowel or stir stick

Kitchen scale that measures in grams

20 g pre-reduced indigo

50 g sodium hydrosulfite

100 g soda ash

4 gallons (15.4 L) cool water

## Directions

**1.** Use the kitchen scale to measure out the pre-reduced indigo, sodium hydrosulfite, and soda ash **(A)**.

**2.** Prepare the vat by filling the container with the cool water.

**3.** Add the soda ash to the water and stir well with the dowel or stir stick; then add the sodium hydrosulfite and stir well. Add the pre-reduced indigo crystals to the mix and stir gently in a circular motion, being careful not to splash or stir vigorously, which will add unwanted oxygen to the vat.

**4.** Once well mixed, change the direction of the stirring and drag the stir stick along the outer edge of the vat before slowly removing it **(B)**. Cover the vat with a lid and let settle for at least 15 minutes and up to 1 hour.

**5.** After the vat has settled, the top of the dyebath will be covered with a layer of foam (this is the flower). The dyebath itself will be a clear yellow or yellow-green color under the flower. Wearing gloves, skim the flower from the top of the vat and place it in the small container **(C)**.

**6.** When you have finished dyeing, put the flower back into the vat and stir it in, once again in a circular motion. Adding the flower back to the vat helps to keep the chemical reaction of the indigo alive. Place the lid tightly on the vat when finished.

## RECALIBRATING THE VAT

If you discover that the liquid has gone more of a gray-blue than yellow-green or is leaving behind blue flecks on your test strip when you check the vat, try adding a small amount of sodium hydrosulfite to get it going again. Dissolve ½ rounded teaspoon (2.5 g) of sodium hydrosulfite in a few tablespoons of warm water and add it to the vat, stir gently, and allow to sit for fifteen minutes before checking again. Repeat as needed until the vat is back to the yellow-green color.

Should the dye color in the vat turn weak and gray in the container or look gray on your fabric when you test it, add more pre-reduced indigo crystals to reinvigorate it. Dissolve 1 to 2 rounded teaspoons (4.5 to 9.5 g) of pre-reduced indigo crystals in a few tablespoons of warm water and add it to the vat. Stir well and wait for fifteen minutes before checking the color again for the bright, yellow-green hue of a healthy vat.

Indigo vats are happiest when they are warm, ideally around 95 to 100°F (35 to 38°C). Wrapping your vat with an electric blanket or a few heating pads can help if you are dyeing in the winter or in a very cold workspace.

## STEP-BY-STEP FOR INDIGO

*This is a quick overview of hand dyeing using indigo. For more detailed instructions, consult the individual projects for specific information. Unlike fiber-reactive dyeing, the indigo process does not require a mordanting step, because the indigo vat already contains all of the necessary chemicals to create a permanent bond with a fiber.*

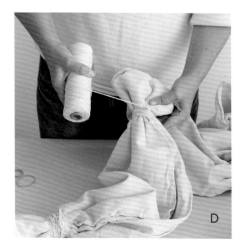

### 1. Scour the Textile

Scour your items or fabric as for the fiber-reactive process (see page 26).

### 2. Add the Resist

When you are tying your fabric, keep in mind that anywhere that the fabric is "tight" it will stay "white" (see a demonstration of this concept in Making Patterns on page 34). The binding medium (such as rubber bands or twine) will resist the dye and leave behind a pattern **(D)**. Anywhere that the fabric is loose and unbound will absorb the indigo dye and become blue.

More white space will result in more of the pattern, if you thoroughly soak your fabric in water before you begin, as the fabric will absorb more water and less dye. Conversely, adding your items to the vat when they are dry will result in patterns that have more blue because the dry fabric is able to absorb more dye. Read more about resist techniques in Making Patterns (see page 34).

## 3. Dip in the Vat

Carefully immerse the item in the vat, allowing it to soak for about 20 to 30 minutes, depending on the size of your item. Small items such as tea towels or tank tops will take less time than large pieces, such as yardage, bedding, or heavier garments. When your items are thoroughly soaked, gently remove them from the vat. Remember to avoid agitating the vat as much as possible to limit the amount of oxygen introduced into it.

## 4. Oxidize

When you remove your items from the indigo vat they will be a bright, electric green **(E)**. They will slowly begin to turn blue as the fiber is hit with the oxygen in the air. This is the magical oxidation process! Repeat the process of adding the items to the vat, removing them, and letting them oxidize for 15 to 20 minutes between dips in the vat; do not untie the resists. The more times the items are dipped into the indigo vat and then allowed to oxidize, the darker and richer the final blue will be.

## 5. Rinse and Dry

When you are happy with the depth of color, untie your work and allow it to oxidize for at least 20 minutes before washing with a professional textile detergent (see page 23) and warm water **(F)**. If using your home washing machine, rinse your textiles well until the water runs clear before washing.

## 6. Dispose of the Vat

When you are done with the vat, you can dispose of it by pouring it down the drain or somewhere outside away from any high traffic areas. Indigo will dye porcelain—which might mean your sink—so exercise caution. You can clean up your container and stir stick with a mild powdered cleanser and clean water.

**NATURAL FIBERS WORK BEST**

Indigo dye works best on natural fibers such as cotton, rayon, silk, linen, and bamboo; it is not suggested for synthetic fabrics. Fabric blends (cotton with spandex, for instance) will not dye as dark as 100% natural fibers because the synthetic fibers in the blend will not absorb the indigo. However, feel free to experiment with fabric blends and see what happens! Some of my favorite pieces have been experiments.

# Making Patterns

While the process of applying color to a plain textile is captivating on its own, creating a pattern during the dyeing process gives your finished product an additional layer of complexity and visual interest. Many of the projects in *Hand Dyed* have patterns that were created by the resist-dyed technique, which is detailed in this section, but there are other ways to create patterns with dye, too. These intriguing, alternative ways to use dye to make patterns—such as stamping with dye or applying it dry from a saltshaker—are shared, as well.

## RESIST-DYED PATTERNS

*You may be familiar with resist dyeing by a more common term, tie-dye. Tie-dye T-shirts (or other items) are folded, pleated, and/or twisted and then bound with thread, twine, rubber bands, or clamps. The bindings compress the fabric and resist the dye. The areas that are left unbound will receive the dye and a pattern is revealed when the binding material is removed and the cloth is unfolded. This simple principle is the basis of resist dyeing.*

In actuality, tie-dye is a variation of ancient Japanese resist techniques called *shibori*, one of the oldest and most diverse approaches to surface design on cloth. The word *shibori* comes from a root word that means "to wring, squeeze, or press." There is an infinite variety of *shibori* patterns that have been developed through the ages. *Itajime shibori* patterns are created by folding the fabric and then clamping it between blocks of wood, thick plastic, or clamps before dyeing. This versatile technique is used in the Shibori Pendant Lamp project on page 121. You will see additional interpretations of *shibori* applied throughout. Another popular pattern is *te-kumo*, in which cones of fabric are folded and then wrapped with thread; they resemble an intricate spider web when complete. For my take on this particular binding technique, see the Night Sky Curtains on page 143.

Pleated, folded, and clamped resist patterns can be very simple to create yet will yield stunning results. If you are curious about the historical applications of *shibori* and do some research, you will be amazed by some of the intricate patterns that ancient artisans were able to create with simple resists, simple folding and binding, and a lot of patience.

## BASIC PATTERN RESISTS

You can experiment with creating an amazing variety of beautiful patterns with resists made from very simple, everyday items that you probably already have in your home. Here are eight of my favorite go-to patterns to get you started. All these will work equally well with fiber-reactive dye or indigo dye, as shown in the examples here. When one of these patterns is used in a project, detailed directions will appear in the instructions so you can replicate my results.

When I am teaching I have a rhyme that I use with my students: "Anywhere that is tight will stay white." See how this little rhyme applies in the photos on page 37; the areas of the cloth that are folded and then wrapped tightly with a rubber band resist the dye, and a lovely alternating pattern results. With the resist concept in mind, you can begin to think about patterns in a new way and see cloth as a three-dimensional object that can be twisted, wrapped, and clamped in infinite ways to create an unlimited assortment of patterns when it is dyed.

# PATTERN LIBRARY

## Accordion Folds

One of my favorite ways to create patterns is with a simple accordion fold. This easy, back-and-forth fold can give you a huge variety of patterns; you start by folding the fabric into a strip that looks like the bellows of an accordion and take it from there.

Binding and tying an accordion-folded item will create a unique striped effect **(A)**. Make a variation by accordion-folding your item from one corner on a diagonal and binding it **(B)**; this leaves gradations of color and organic lines when dyed and unwrapped. The humble accordion fold is the basis for many of the patterns used here. Have fun with this simple-to-execute design: For instance, experiment with varying the size of the folds—the smaller your folds, the smaller and more intricate your patterns will be.

A

### DIP AND DYE

Try new folds using paper instead of fabric. This fun way to experiment with patterns and colors is also a technique that children love to do—the process is called *orizomegami*. All it involves is folding paper into strips and dipping the ends into shallow containers of watercolor or food coloring, which seeps into the paper. When you use multiple colors, each in its own container, a kaleidoscope of patterns and hues results from the colors bleeding into one another. Give it a try! See the Orizomegami Wrapping Paper project on page 59 for more information.

B

## Scrunch

Another one of my favorite patterns is what I like to call the "scrunch." To create this freeform pattern, lay your fabric flat on a clean work surface and gather it all together, scrunching it into a flat, somewhat even puck shape, then secure it with more or less evenly spaced rubber bands **(C)**. The more tightly you secure the rubber bands, the more white space you will see in your final design. I love this pattern because it is so simple, yet it creates amazing crystal-like designs on all kinds of fabric. For a neat variation, pinch a spot of fabric and twist it into a spiral before scrunching the excess fabric around it—incredible swirl patterns will result. You can see this pattern in all its glory in the Super Bloom Robe project on page 101.

C

## Twists

To create these undulating patterns, hold one end of the fabric and begin to twist it tightly as if you were wringing out a towel. Continue to wring the fabric until the entire length has twisted into a knot **(D)**. Secure the textile with twine or rubber bands so the twists stay in place in the dyebath. The more tightly the fabric is twisted, the more white will appear in the final pattern; the more loosely it is twisted, the more dye will absorb into the fabric, resulting in deeper colors on the final project. The Cozy Newborn Wrap on page 57 shows this pattern dyed in a warm gray.

D

## Itajime Triangle

Many simple, geometric *shibori* patterns are made from a strip of accordion-folded fabric that is accordion-folded a second time into grids or triangles and then bound with clamps. The width of the initial accordion fold will determine the size of the final pattern. For this *itajime* variation, accordion-fold the fabric and then fold one end of the accordion over to create a triangle. Fold the triangle back and forth as neatly as possible to create a stack of accordion-folded triangles. Place wooden boards, canning jar lids, or cut plastic on both sides of the stack and at the center, and clamp them tightly in place **(E)**. Experiment not only with the size and shape of the boards and clamps, but also by placing the clamped resist off center or on one edge, or change the size of the boards and clamps that bind the stacked triangle. These tweaks will create new patterns.

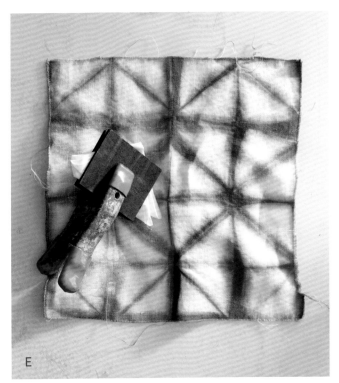

E

## Itajime Grid

For this *itajime* variation, accordion-fold the fabric as for the Itajime Triangle pattern, but fold one end of the accordion up to create a square or rectangle rather than a triangle. After folding the entire strip, place a resist on both sides of the center of the grid stack, and clamp tightly into place **(F)**. This process results in a rather orderly collection of squares. You can change it up by moving the position of the clamp to a different area or changing the resists as suggested for the Itajime Triangle pattern.

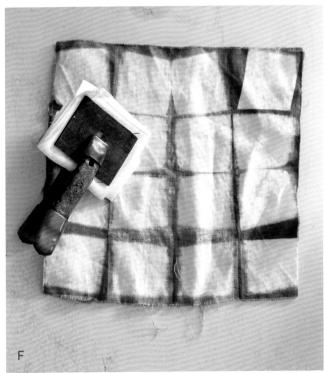

F

## Circles

Make organic-looking circles by gathering the fabric at a point and securing the pinch with a rubber band or winding with twine (**G**). You can use a small rock, coin, or even a bean at the tip of the fabric before securing the rubber band around the base of the object. When the resist is applied around a circular object such as a coin, it helps to create more even dot shapes. To make a solid white polka dot, use a piece of plastic to cover the tip of the fabric and secure it in place with a rubber band and twine, making sure that no dye can penetrate the plastic wrap. (See how this pattern was applied in the Simple Swaddling Blankets on page 63.) For concentric circles over the whole of the fabric (**H**), gather the entire piece of fabric from a single point and then wrap rubber bands or twine around the length of your fabric.

G

These are just a few pattern ideas to get you started with resist dyeing; I cannot emphasize enough how magical this process can be. Set yourself free from any worry about your patterns, enjoy the process of binding your fabric, and let the dye do the rest! You may want to begin by simply wadding up a scrap of fabric into a ball, wrapping it with a rubber band, and placing it in the dye—then see what happens. Each piece you dye and each pattern you try will teach you something new. The more you experiment with resist dyeing, the more you will learn, and the more sophisticated your patterns will become.

H

## STAMPED PATTERNS

*A few of the projects here have patterns created in an entirely different way—by stamping. For a lovely example of hand-stamping combined with solid-color dyeing, see the Classic Patchwork Quilt on page 151. Each stamping project in part 2 will have specific instructions, but here is some basic information to keep in mind when you want to create a hand-stamped pattern using dye. Note that this stamping method is not suitable for use with indigo—fiber-reactive dye is required.*

To begin, be sure to scour (see page 26) and mordant the fiber (see page 27) before stamping. I suggest that you allow the cloth to dry with the mordant still on the fibers, so do not rinse the textile. Stamping on a dry prepared surface will keep the fine lines of the stamp from bleeding and becoming fuzzy as they would on a wet surface.

Create a concentrated slurry (see page 19) of fiber-reactive dye and then sprinkle a tiny amount (about ¼ teaspoon [1.2 g]) of sodium alginate (a stabilizer and emulsifier extracted from seaweed) on the top of the slurry; stir to dissolve **(A)**. The sodium alginate thickens the dye, allowing it to cling more evenly to the surface of the stamp and to create a cleaner print. Add only a very small amount of sodium alginate at a time, as it will continue to thicken as time passes and can become gooey if too much is added. Use the project instructions as your guide for this step. This process works well for hand painting with dye on textiles, too!

Pour out the thickened slurry onto a stack of several paper towels, layered to make a dye "stamp pad" **(B)**. It is a good idea to place the stamp pad on top of a piece of plastic or an old plate to keep the liquid from dyeing the surface below.

Place the stamp down flat onto the surface of the pad and coat the stamp with an even layer of thickened dye by pressing it into the stamp, repeating as needed. I usually make a test print on a clean rag or paper towel to make sure that everything looks good before moving on to the prepared fabric **(C)**.

Press the entire surface of the stamp evenly with the heel of your hand, being careful not to let it shift during the process **(D)**. Add more dye to the pad as needed.

When you are finished stamping the pattern, allow the dye to sit on the fabric and cure for at least twenty-four hours before washing out the cloth. I like to let pieces cure on a drying rack, or I layer the stamped pieces in between pieces of clean newsprint to prevent smudging.

## STENCILED PATTERNS

*In a twist on traditional dyeing, I've experimented with creating patterns by removing color instead of adding it. In a couple of projects, including the Points of Light Pillows on page 123 and the Mud Cloth Chair on page 147, I first dyed the item but then applied a bleach paste through a stencil to remove color in a systematic way. It can be just as rewarding to create a pattern in this "reverse" way of working.*

The basic procedure involves making a stencil from plastic stencil film or Mylar and cutting a pattern into it using a craft knife. After your textile has been dyed, washed, and dried, the bleach paste is prepared and worked through the stencil with a brush **(A)**. For more detailed information about this patternmaking technique, see one of the projects mentioned above.

## DRY DYE PATTERNS

When you apply dry dye powder to a prepared textile, you can create gorgeous organic patterns with colors that flow into one another. It's about as simple as dyeing can get—dry dye is shaken over the item until you're satisfied with the results. Dye powder can also be applied over ice and allowed to slowly melt onto the fabric below, creating fabulous colorscapes. See these techniques in play in the Confetti Quilt on page 129 and the Sunrise Blouse on page 83. When playing with the ice dyeing process, keep careful notes of the order in which you add the dyes to your project. Layering colors in a different order can totally change the finished outcome.

### MAKING GRADATIONS

There is an interesting technique called low-water immersion dyeing that uses as little water as possible; this method allows the dye to slowly blend and creep through the fabric, creating beautiful colors and gradations. To try it, you need a container in which your textile will just fit when tightly scrunched or crumpled, which forms a resist effect against the dye. This is yet another example of the diverse ways that patterns can be formed with dye. As you can see, there are endless possibilities when creating patterns on cloth. Allow yourself the artistic freedom to experiment and be sure to record your results; this will help you re-create a favorite pattern later. The final section in part 1 details color (see page 44), giving you one more tool to use when you explore hand dyeing.

# Playing with Color

I love to play with color, and I enjoy the triumphs, as well as the failures, that come from experimenting with new hues, because I always learn something valuable. But everyone may not have the time or inclination to learn by trial and error, so all the projects in *Hand Dyed* include exact color recipes for precisely this reason. But if you are excited by playing with custom colors and want to mix your own, I would like to share some of the knowledge that I have gained, which will help you in your exploration of color.

These swatches demonstrate the versatility of combining colors in various ways. Colors can also be layered by putting them in a dyebath of one transparent color first, and then in a second transparent color. Note the variation in color that results from beginning with one shade as opposed to the other; for example, the orange swatch at far left was dipped in magenta first, and then in yellow.

## COLOR BASICS

Before getting into the specifics about mixing color, I begin with a little background about color theory. Keep these concepts in mind as you read through the rest of this section; they are the foundation of the techniques I share throughout.

The traditional primary colors—red, yellow, and blue—are the starting points for mixing colors when working with paints and other pigments, but dyes are transparent, so they blend together much differently. When working with dyes, the primary colors are magenta (a hot pink), yellow, cyan, and black, which can be used to mix and layer an amazing array of vibrant hues **(A)**. Identifying color temperature—whether a shade is warm or cool—is also very important when mixing colors. See Warm or Cool? on page 47 for more information.

It is also helpful to understand the concepts of tone, tint, and shade. You may be familiar with these terms as they are applied to fine art painting. A tint is a color with white added to it. Tints are commonly referred to as pastels and are colors that are lighter and less saturated. Tones are created when both black and white are added to a color. Tones can be lighter or darker than the original color, depending on the ratio of black to white that is added. Tones are deeper and more complex than tints. Shades are created when black is added to the color. Because black is so intense, very little is needed to change the color into a shade. With dye, changes in tone, tint, and shade are achieved differently than with paint, as you will learn on the following pages.

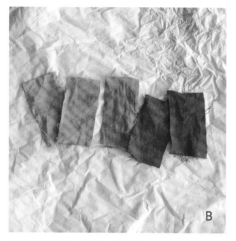

## MIXING CUSTOM SHADES

Getting exactly the color that you have in mind when you are hand dyeing can sometimes difficult, and mixing custom shades can be even harder. Unlike paint, dyes do not always exhibit their final color—dye in powdered form is very often a completely different color in the container than it is after it is dissolved in water. For example, gray dyes can look pale pink in the container. But when the powdered dye is dissolved in water, it transforms into a translucent version of the color.

The color changes again when it touches the fiber you are using. Rayon will take the dye differently than linen or cotton, because each fiber will naturally pull out different parts of the dye as the chemical reactions take place between the fiber and the dye. Time changes the color yet again—the longer you soak the material, the more saturated the final color will be (B). And finally, after curing, rinsing, washing, and drying, the final color of your hand-dyed piece is revealed (C). Throughout that journey there can be a lot of changes and surprises. There is often a lot of experimentation to end up with the exact color you have in your mind's eye when you embark on a project.

I cannot stress enough how important it is to test your materials and your colors when blending custom hues or layering colors (dyeing in one color first, then a second). I keep a basket full of fabric strips in my workspace to test colors. When I get new dye colors or am trying a new blend, I set up small test batches (about 2 cups [480 ml] of water to ¼ teaspoon [1.2 g] dye is a good ratio) and let the bottom half of a fabric strip soak in the bath for twenty-five or thirty minutes (D). As the dye wicks up the fabric you can get a sense of the overall tone and undertones of the color. Is it warm or cool? Some colors are very cool and have undertones of blue and cyan, other colors have a warm tone that will bring up pinks or yellows. Write the color on the test strips with a fine-point permanent pen to use as a reference when you are mixing colors and for inspiration. Or tape a piece of your test strip to the top of a dye jar so you have an easy visual reference for each color (E). I love to mix and match these color tests as I look for color story ideas.

## WARM OR COOL?

Color theory is a fascinating field. Colors can make you feel warmer or cooler, and even change your mood. For the purposes of dyeing, defining a color as warm or cool can be made simple: Warm colors are in the red, orange, and yellow families—think of heat or sunlight—while cool colors, such as blue or green, are reminiscent of the ocean and the sky. Keeping these nature references in mind helps characterize the colors that you mix.

## TIPS FOR CREATING CUSTOM COLORS

I find it much easier to mix colors once I have identified them individually as warm or cool. Once I've made that determination, I begin to experiment with more confidence. Here are several of the approaches I take when I create my own custom colors.

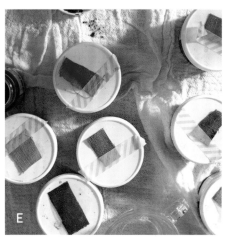

### Adding warmth to a cool color

I like to make this change to a color by starting with a warm base. Instead of starting with plain water to get a nice warm pink, for instance, I will mix a dyebath with a color such as Procion MX Ecru as my starting point, and then add the desired amount of pink dye. The yellow-based ecru creates the perfect foundation for mixing a custom shade of warm, peachy pink.

### Adding coolness to a warm color

This is the same process as adding warmth above, except you would begin with a base color on the opposite end of the spectrum, such as Procion MX Neutral Gray, which is a cool, pale gray.

### Adding overall depth

I often mix three dyes in the same color family together to yield deeper and more nuanced colors than can be achieved with just a single color of dye. For instance, you can achieve incredible deep blues and greens by mixing a green, a cyan, and a blue dye together **(F)**.

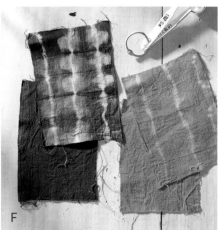

### Making a tint

When you make a tint with dye, it is done by mixing a less-saturated dyebath or exposing the item to less time in the dyebath.

### Making a tone

Tones are easily mixed by adding a bit of a warm or cool gray dye to a premixed color. This technique gives a lot of depth without adding a lot of color. You can also achieve tones with dye by adding another color in the

same color family that is a little bit darker or lighter, such as mixing ocher into yellow or cobalt into aquamarine. This makes the dye more saturated and is fun to play with if you are looking for very bright, exuberant colors.

## Making a shade

Mixing shades is similar to mixing tones, but the end result is deeper and darker. I like to mix shades by adding a tiny bit of black or gray dye to a color or adding the same color in a deeper, more complex hue—or sometimes a little bit of both. Photo **G** illustrates the concepts of tint, tone, and shade in relation to the original color.

## Increasing the intensity

If you want to bump up the intensity of a color, consider adding cyan, yellow, or magenta. Just a tiny bit of lemon yellow added to a premixed yellow or green dye will make it brighter and more vibrant, cyan will add a pop of bright blue to green and blues, and magenta will brighten any pink or red.

## TIPS FOR SUCCESS

*I hope you are excited to move on to part 2 where you can incorporate all you've learned about dyes, fabrics, patterns, and color to make a variety of wonderful projects to use, wear, and enjoy. Here are some final tips before you set up your dye studio:*

• Properly scour the fibers before dyeing. One of the most common reasons for uneven and undesirable results is the starches and other residue that remain on the fabric or yarn, which keep the dye from penetrating the fibers. Preparing the fiber properly will help ensure success.

• Make sure that items are thoroughly soaked in the mordant before dyeing. A good rule of thumb is to wait until the fiber no longer floats on top of the bath. If the fiber sinks under the surface of the soda ash bath, you can assume that the solution has penetrated deep into the fibers and the item is ready to dye.

• Test your materials! Make sure to test new colors and patterns before using them on a large project. I like to try out new colors or pattern ideas on cotton napkins, tea towels, or pillowcases. I prefer to test new ideas on useful items that can come home with me or be given as gifts.

• Keep your tools, resists, and work areas clean. One speck of dye from your work surface or on your stir stick can leave unwanted dye marks that are difficult or impossible to remove from your next project.

• Be prepared when working on a large scale. Large, bulky projects (such as the Indigo Stripe Hammock on page 77 or the Sunshine Play Tent on page 73) are rated as more difficult primarily because they absorb such a large amount of dye and become very heavy. Have a plan and gather all your supplies before you start working, because wet textiles can be very heavy! To make large items easier to handle, wring out as much dye as possible from them before the wrapping and curing steps.

• Read the back of each new dye color for special instructions. Some colors work best in hot water (such as black), and others should only be used with cold water. Be sure to confirm the proper water temperature before starting a project.

• Each project was designed to teach valuable dyeing skills and yield almost foolproof results, but as you branch out on your own and begin to play with custom colors and new blends, there can be missteps along the way. If you get frustrated, keep going and do not quit! I have dyed many unattractive items, but each one has taught me something. Every "mistake" is an opportunity to learn and grow as an artist. And when in doubt, throw it in the indigo vat!

## INSPIRATION FROM NATURE

Most often, I find inspiration for color combinations in the natural world. Mother Nature has the incredible ability to mix outrageous colors together in the most inspiring way! If you take the time to really look at a flower or a leaf, you will often see an intriguing array of surprising colors. Tulips can turn from pale green to soft pink to electric orange in the most subtle and magical ways. When you open your eyes to color and begin to truly see as opposed to just looking, you will be amazed by the color combinations that are possible. Take a walk and bring back photos, specimens, or sketches of some of the treasures you find in nature—they will be an invaluable resource as you continue to experiment with color.

PART 2

# PROJECTS

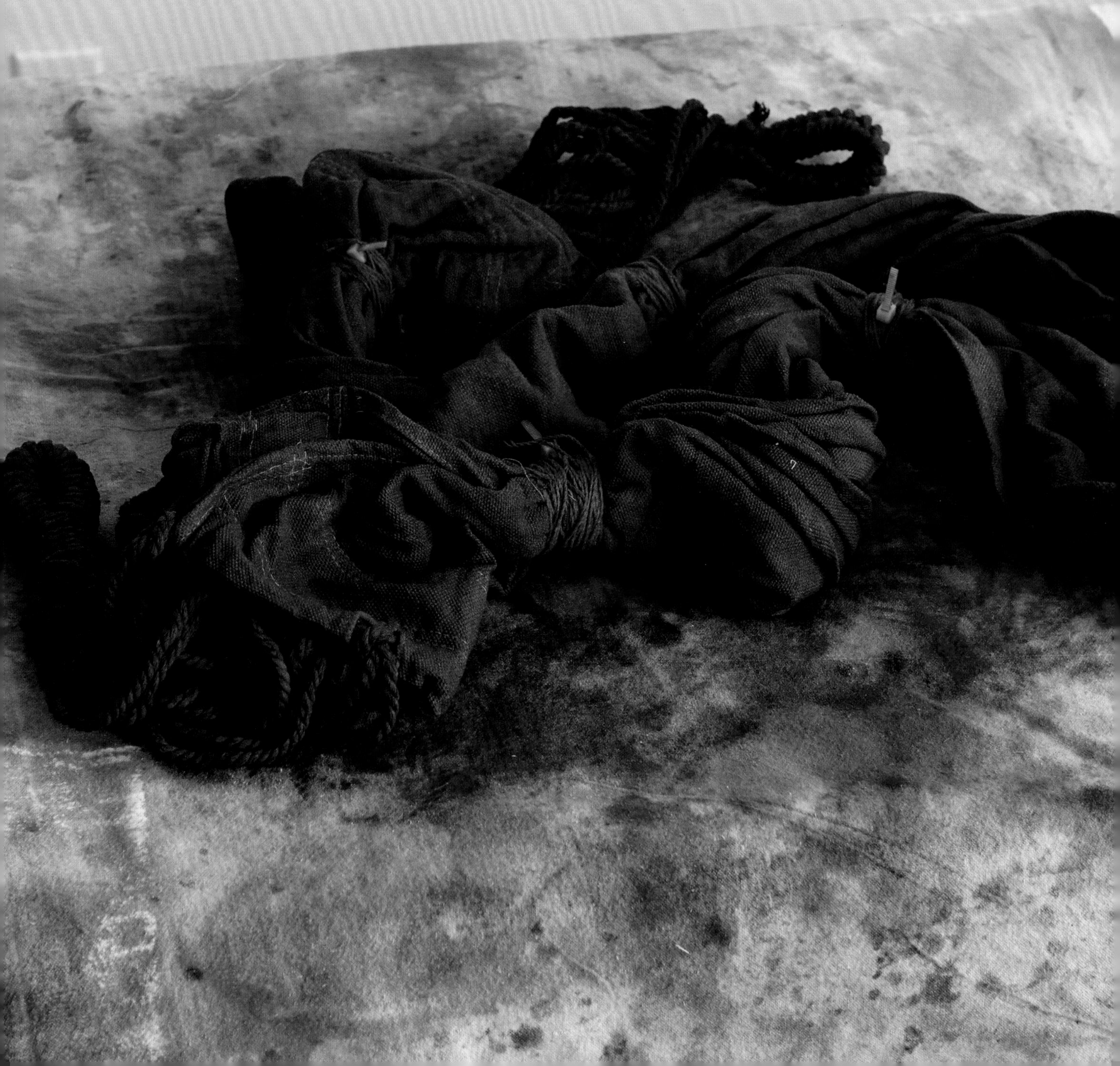

FOR YOUR FAMILY

# Cozy Newborn Wrap

*I loved wearing my babies in a wrap when they were newborns. This cotton wrap is a perfect gift for a new parent and it's a great project to breathe new life into an infant wrap that has seen better days. I found this creamy cotton wrap at a consignment store and dyed it a chic and gender-neutral warm gray. This pattern is as simple as you can get, making it easy to work with such a long piece of stretchy fabric.*

## SUPPLIES

Dyer's Kit (see page 20), including a wide 5-gallon (19 L) plastic container

100% cotton baby wrap (you can make your own, as well—look for simple patterns online)

Soda ash soak (see page 27)

Fiber-reactive dye in gray and tan (I used Procion MX Neutral Gray and Ecru)

4 gallons (15.4 L) of warm water

| LEVEL: | SKILLS LEARNED: | FIBER: | DYE: |
|---|---|---|---|
| ●○○○ | Tub dyeing, twisting, adding resists, mixing custom colors | Cellulose (cotton knit) | Fiber-reactive dye |

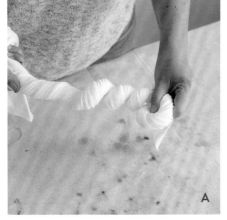

A

B

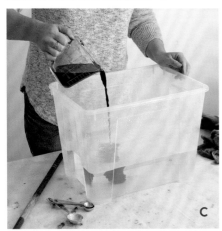

C

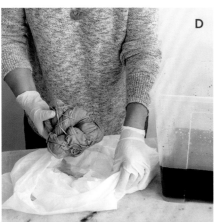

D

## DIRECTIONS

**1.** Scour the wrap (see page 26). When you're ready to dye, find a friend if you can—this particular pattern is easier to execute with two people. Have your friend firmly hold one end of the wrap while you pull it taut. Begin to twist until it becomes tight and the twists begin to fold over on themselves. If you are working alone, secure one end of the wrap on a doorknob or a sturdy hook to twist it **(A)**.

**2.** When the wrap is entirely twisted, secure it in place with rubber bands **(B)**. Immerse the bundle in the prepared soda ash soak until fully saturated (at least 30 minutes).

**3.** While the wrap is soaking, prepare the dyebath. Fill a 5-gallon (19 L) plastic container with 4 gallons (15.4 L) warm water. Wearing your safety gear, make a slurry (see page 19) in a measuring container: add 3 rounded teaspoons (14 g) of gray dye and 2 rounded teaspoons (9.5 g) of tan dye to about ½ cup (120 ml) of warm water. When the mixture is smooth and the dye has fully dissolved, add it to the container to create the dyebath **(C)**.

**4.** Wring out any excess water from the baby wrap and put it in the dyebath. Soak for 1 hour, setting a timer if desired. Stir the wrap every 15 to 20 minutes.

**5.** After 1 hour, remove the wrap from the dye and wring any excess dye back into the bucket. If a darker color is desired, allow the wrap to soak for longer, checking the color every 30 minutes—soak for up to 4 hours for the deepest color. Note that the wrap shown here was in the dyebath for a total of about 75 minutes.

**6.** Place the baby wrap in a plastic bag **(D)** and allow to cure overnight or up to 24 hours for the richest color and sharpest patterns.

**7.** After the wrap has cured, unwrap, discard the rubber bands, and rinse in cold water until the water runs clear. Machine-wash in hot water with a PTD and machine-dry.

# Orizomegami Wrapping Paper

*For this colorful project, you will learn* orizomegami, *the Japanese art of folding and dyeing paper. I offer two variations of this project, which is an easy, versatile way to play with new pattern and color combinations. This is an excellent project to enjoy with children! Make sure you have lots of extra rice paper on hand—orizomegami is so fun to make you won't want to stop once you start. Leftover sheets of paper can be used for collage, book arts, or any other paper craft.*

## SUPPLIES

Dyer's Kit (see page 20), including shallow containers for each color

Liquid watercolors in several different colors (I used Dr. Ph. Martin's Radiant Water Color Concentrate in Ice Pink, Yellow Ocher, Tobacco Brown, and Violet)

2 tablespoons (30 ml) of water per container

2 cups (480 ml) of clean water

36 × 24" (90 × 60 cm) sheets of rice paper, as many as desired

Bone folder (optional)

| LEVEL: | SKILLS LEARNED: | FIBER: | DYE: |
|---|---|---|---|
| ●○○○ | Folding, adding resists, color layering | Cellulose (rice paper) | Liquid Watercolor |

## VARIATION 1

**1.** Cover your work surface with a large sheet (or sheets) of newsprint. Add 2 tablespoons (30 ml) water to each of the three shallow containers. Add 6 to 12 drops of liquid watercolor to the water in each container, depending on how saturated you want your colors—I suggest experimenting with how much pigment you add to the water before you begin working on your project paper. Have a jar of clean water and a roll of paper towels or clean rags ready on your work surface. Set the dyes aside.

**2.** Accordion-fold a sheet of rice paper lengthwise at 1½" (4 cm) intervals; if it is helpful, use a bone folder to help smooth the folds. Fold up the bottom corner of the paper to create a triangle. Continue folding back and forth until the entire sheet is stacked into a triangle **(A)**. Hold the folds in place with a clothespin.

**3.** Dip one of the long bottom corners of the triangle into the yellow watercolor and hold it there until the color begins to absorb into the folded paper. Allow the paint to wick about 1" (2.5 cm) into the paper. Add more water and watercolor to the container as needed. Repeat to dip the opposite long bottom corner in the yellow paint.

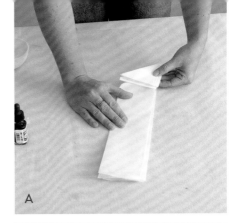

A

**4.** When the first color has absorbed, rotate the triangle and dip the short top corner into the violet watercolor and allow it to wick into the paper as in step 3. Remove the clothespin, if you prefer.

**5.** Dip each of the three points of the triangle into the brown watercolor, one at a time, until the pigment begins to wick into and blend with the yellow and violet **(B)**.

**6.** Set the folded paper on a paper towel or clean rag and allow to sit and dry slightly. Repeat for the desired number of sheets. See step 3 of Variation 2 for finishing instructions.

B

## VARIATION 2

**1.** Prepare this variation as in step 1 of Variation 1, but use only two containers. Accordion-fold a sheet of rice paper into 1½" (4 cm) intervals and then fold the paper into rectangles. Hold the folds in place with a clothespin.

**2.** Dip both short ends of the rectangle into the pink watercolor and allow it to saturate the paper. Repeat with the violet watercolor **(C)**. Set the folded paper on a paper towel and let dry slightly. Repeat for the desired number of sheets.

C

**3.** Gently unfold the damp paper, being careful not to stretch or rip it, and hang it from a drying rack. You can also allow the papers to dry flat, placing each sheet between sheets of clean newsprint **(D)**. Allow the paper to dry completely, for several hours or overnight.

## TIP

This *orizomegami* rice paper project can easily be modified in color or scale. Have fun experimenting with different folding techniques or layering the colors in a different order for totally new results.

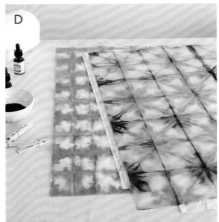

D

# Simple Swaddling Blankets

*These hand-dyed swaddling blankets are a thoughtful offering for a new or expecting mother, and rich indigo blue is a beautiful, timeless color choice for either girls or boys. I offer two different patterns for this project. The itajime shibori style used in Variation 1 is a beautiful example of simple folding and clamping. Variation 2, which features a bound-and-capped design, results in pretty white circles and crisp polka dots. Both are timeless motifs that are perfect for children; indigo-dyed cotton decorated with a shibori pattern is a traditional gift for newborns in Japan.*

## SUPPLIES

Dyer's Kit (see page 20), including a 5-gallon (19 L) bucket

Cotton gauze swaddling blankets, each approximately 47 × 47" (117.5 × 117.5 cm) — as many as desired

Small wooden or plastic blocks for Variation 1, approximately 4 × 3" (10 × 7.5 cm)

Large C-clamp

Container to hold several gallons (liters) of clean water

Indigo kit (see Resources, page 158) or indigo vat (see page 30)

Plastic wrap or sandwich bags for Variation 2

## DYER'S NOTES

The cotton gauze blankets used in this project are very fluffy, and they will not fold perfectly. Do not worry, just do the best you can to wrangle them into a pleasing shape; the resulting pattern will still be beautiful.

| LEVEL: | SKILLS LEARNED: | FIBER: | DYE: |
|---|---|---|---|
| ●○○○ | Vat dyeing, folding, adding resists, dyeing with indigo | Cellulose (cotton) | Indigo |

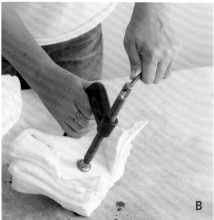

## DIRECTIONS

### VARIATION 1

**1.** Scour (see page 26) and hang or machine-dry the blanket(s). Lay the gauze blanket out on a large table or the floor and fold it in half lengthwise, then accordion-fold the blanket into a long stack of fabric about 6 to 8" (15 to 20 cm) wide. Starting at one end, fold the corner over to create a triangle, then fold the triangle back onto itself, accordion-style. Repeat until you have a neatly folded stack of fabric **(A)**.

**2.** Use rubber bands to hold the bundle in place—or have a friend help you—and then place a C-clamp over the blocks and fasten tightly to sandwich the blocks around the fabric **(B)**. This is the Itajime Triangle pattern (see page 39).

**3.** After binding, soak the blanket in a container filled with several gallons (liters) of plain water until it is fully saturated, at least 15 minutes.

**4.** Remove the blanket from the bucket and squeeze out as much excess water as possible without disturbing the position of the blocks and clamp.

**5.** Place just the tip of the triangle into the dyebath (roughly 2½" [6.25 cm] from the tip of the triangle) and let it sit in the indigo for 4 to 7 minutes **(C)**.

**6.** Remove the tip of the triangle, squeeze out the extra dye, and flip the triangle over. Now dip the long edge of the triangle into the dye (roughly 2½" [6.25 cm] from the edge) for 4 to 7 minutes as in step 5. Repeat the process of dyeing both the tip and edge of the blanket, letting each side oxidize (see page 33) fully between being submerged in the dyebath, until the desired shade of blue is achieved **(D)**. For this project variation, the process was repeated four times.

**7.** Squeeze out any excess dye and remove the clamps and boards. Unfold the blanket and hang to oxidize until all the lines in the pattern have fully turned indigo blue. To finish, see step 6 of Variation 2.

## VARIATION 2

**1.** Scour (see page 26) and hang or machine-dry the blanket(s). For this pattern, you will create circles and polka dots (see page 40). Wrap the cotton gauze tightly with a rubber band to create circles; for crisp, white polka dots, cap the end with a cut piece of plastic wrap so the dye cannot penetrate. See the instructions for the Night Sky Curtains on page 143 to learn how to plot out the circles and dots in an even pattern or, as shown here, just create the pattern as you go!

**2.** Lay the gauze blanket out on a large table or the floor. For the circle pattern, pinch a cone of fabric and bind it with a rubber band about 3" (7.5 cm) from the peak of the fabric.

**3.** To create polka dots, follow step 2 above, but then take piece of plastic (small snack bags or cut squares of plastic wrap about 7" [17.5 cm] square) and cover the top of the fabric that is exposed **(E)**. Secure again tightly with a second rubber band **(F)**.

**4.** Repeat all over the surface of the blanket, alternating capped and uncapped resists, until the entire blanket has been bound.

**5.** Soak the blanket in plain water until fully saturated, at least 15 minutes. Remove the blanket from the bucket and squeeze out as much excess water as possible without disturbing the bound plastic or rubber bands.

**6.** Submerge the bound blanket in the vat. Let it soak for at least 15 minutes and then remove from the vat, gently squeezing out as much dye as possible without disturbing the pattern. Allow the indigo to oxidize (with rubber bands and plastic caps in place) in between dips in the vat until the desired shade of blue is achieved. For a darker shade of indigo, repeat the process several times.

**7.** Rinse with cold water until the water runs clear and then machine-wash in hot water with a PTD following the directions on page 24. Machine-wash and dry with like colors.

### TIP

Instead of using blocks for Variation 1, try canning jar lids for a *shibori* pattern that has softer, floral shapes and circles instead of squares or rectangles. Do not be afraid to experiment with the shape of the resists you use—it can result in beautiful and unexpected patterns!

# Festive Cotton Buntings

*These decorative buntings are simple to put together and will bring a bit of color and rich texture to any room. I love these for any kind of party, but they're also great as full-time decor, especially for a child's space. This project comes together quickly. Enlist your young ones to help with the tying—children love to work on these colorful, shaggy buntings.*

## SUPPLIES

Dyer's Kit (see page 20), including one wide 5-gallon (19 L) container for each color

2 yards (1.8 m) of white quilter's cotton or muslin, 56" (140 cm) wide

2 cups (454 g) of soda ash for a dip-dyed bunting, or soda ash soak (see page 27) for a solid-color bunting

Fiber-reactive dyes in coral, purple, and raspberry (I used Procion MX in Coral Pink, Eggplant Purple, and Raspberry)

4 gallons (15.4 L) of warm water for a solid-color bunting or 2 gallons (7.6 L) of warm water for a dip-dyed bunting

Soft cotton rope or macramé cord, at least 3 yards (2.75 m) per bunting

## NOTE

2 yards (1.8 m) of fabric per color yields a finished bunting that is 4 to 5' (1.2 to 1.5 m) long; buy more yardage if you want multiple buntings.

| LEVEL: | SKILLS LEARNED: | FIBER: | DYE: |
|---|---|---|---|
| ●○○○ | Tub dyeing, dip dyeing | Cellulose (cotton) | Fiber-reactive dye |

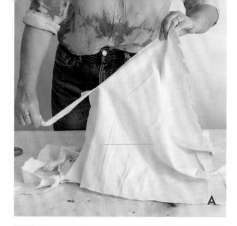

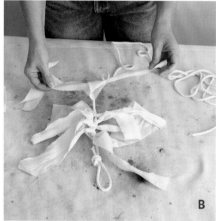

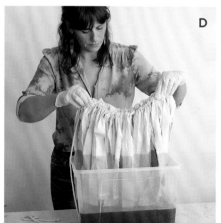

## DIP-DYED BUNTINGS

**1.** Cut a 6 to 7' (1.8 to 2.1 m) length of the rope and tie a slip knot at one end, leaving a loop. This loop will later be used to hang the banner. Secure the loop over a hook or doorknob.

**2.** Iron the cotton yardage smooth. Using the tip of sharp scissors, make ½" (1.3 cm) deep cuts in the selvedge edge of the cotton every 1 to 1½" (2.5 to 4 cm) along the length of the piece. Tear the cotton at the snip marks, making at least ten strips in each batch **(A)**. Cut those strips of cotton into 14 to 16" (35 to 40 cm) lengths—if the strips are much longer, they will be prone to tangling. That said, you can experiment with longer pieces of cotton to make a great wall hanging or fringe for a doorway.

**3.** Tie the first strip of cotton near the knot and continue until the bunting is your desired length **(B)**.

**4.** To make a "flat" fringe bunting, line up all the knots in a row and use your fingers to "comb" the strips in one direction **(C)**. For a "shaggy" bunting, use your hands to twist the cotton around the rope and shake it out for more of a pompom effect, as you see in the photo on page 66.

**5.** Make the dyebath using 2 gallons (7.6 L) of warm water, 2 cups (454 g) of soda ash, and a slurry (see page 19) of 3 rounded teaspoons (14 g) of coral dye. Stir well. I used a wide container for this project to accommodate the width of the bunting.

**6.** Fold the bunting in half so it's more manageable, and slowly dip it into the container until the color has wicked about three-quarters of the way up the bunting **(D)**. Pull the bunting up slowly and allow the bottom ends to soak in the dyebath for 10 to 20 minutes; this creates an ombré effect, with the pink more intense at the bottom.

**7.** After about 10 minutes (or when the cotton is your desired color), remove the bunting from the bath and wring out as much excess dye as possible. Rinse the cotton strips by hand until the water runs clear, then swish them in a light bath (about a capful) of PTD, combing them with your fingers to keep the strips from getting tangled during washing; rinse carefully. Wring out as much water as possible and hang to dry. Smooth out any wrinkles with a garment steamer or a steam iron on the cotton setting.

### TIP

For a stronger color on the ombré bunting, carefully wrap it in a plastic bag and allow to cure for 12 to 24 hours before hand-washing in step 7.

## DIRECTIONS

### SOLID-COLOR BUNTINGS

**1.** Prepare the cotton yardage for dyeing by scouring and cutting it into 2-yard (1.8 m) lengths (if necessary). Submerge in the soda ash soak for at least 20 minutes and up to several hours.

**2.** While the cotton is soaking, prepare the dyebaths wearing your safety gear. Use a 5-gallon (19 L) container filled with 4 gallons (15.4 L) of warm water and 3 rounded teaspoons (14 g) of dye for each individual color. Stir well to remove any dry clumps of dye before adding the presoaked fabric.

**3.** When the cotton is fully saturated in the soda ash soak, wring out any excess liquid into the bucket and add the cotton to the dyebath. Stir well to make sure it is fully submerged, and soak for at least 1 hour—up to 4 hours for the most intense color. Stir frequently.

**4.** After the cotton has reached your desired shade, remove it from the dye and wring out any excess. Wrap in a plastic bag and allow to cure for 12 to 24 hours before rinsing and washing with PTD (see page 24); machine-dry. To tear into strips and arrange these on the rope, follow steps 1–4 shown for dip-dyed buntings (see opposite).

### DYER'S NOTES

If you're making solid-color buntings and the color is not totally even on the fabric, don't worry. The cotton is going to be torn into smaller pieces, and any variation in the color will only add more depth and interest to the final piece.

# Silk Ribbons

*I love this project because it is so simple yet so versatile. These colorful ribbons can be used to wrap gorgeous gifts or would be a stunning project for wedding decor. I like to keep spools of white silk ribbon on hand and add a batch to a dyebath when I am working on new colors. This twisted-and-clamped pattern is very simple, but feel free to try other binding techniques. Folding the ribbon into shapes or wrapping it with rubber bands or twine before dyeing will also create intriguing, unique patterns.*

## SUPPLIES

Dyer's Kit (see page 20), including wooden clothespins or other small clamps and a 1-pint (500 ml) plastic or glass container for each dye color

15-yard (13.7 m) spool of silk ribbon, 1 to 1½" (2.5 to 4 cm) wide (rayon ribbon will also work)

Soda ash soak (see page 27)

2 cups (480 ml) of room-temperature water per container

1 tablespoon (17 g) of dyer's salt per container (optional)

Fiber-reactive dye in the colors of your choice (I used Procion MX in Peach, Jet Black, Carmine Red, and Golden Yellow, and Dharma Fiber Reactive Dye in Forest Green, Light Pink, Strong Navy, and Mist Gray)

2 cups (480 ml) plain water

## DYER'S NOTES

Acid dyes are made specifically for silk and other protein fibers, but I used fiber-reactive dyes for this project because I wanted the colors to be a little more muted. Feel free to explore dyeing silk ribbon with acid dye, as well—it will produce very bright, saturated colors and ultra-crisp patterns.

| LEVEL: | SKILLS LEARNED: | FIBER: | DYE: |
|---|---|---|---|
| ●○○○ | Adding resists, small-batch dyeing | Protein (silk) | Fiber-reactive dye (see Dyer's Notes) |

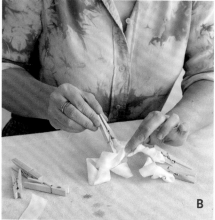

## DIRECTIONS

**1.** Unspool a length of silk ribbon; I suggest working with 3 to 5 yards (2.8 to 4.6 m) at a time. To scour, hand-wash the ribbon in room-temperature water with a capful of PTD and allow to air-dry.

**2.** Wrap the ribbon loosely into 12" (30 cm) lengths **(A)**.

**3.** Twist the ribbon every 2 to 3" (5 to 7.5 cm) and secure with a wooden clothespin, placing it over the twist **(B)**. After the twists are pinned, soak the ribbon in the prepared soda ash bath for at least 10 minutes (longer is fine).

**4.** While the ribbon is soaking, don your safety gear and add 2 cups (480 L) of room-temperature tap water to each of your containers, along with 1 tablespoon (17 g) of dyer's salt. To each container, add ½ level teaspoon (2.5 g) of dye and stir well so that there are no lumps of dye and the mixture is smooth.

**5.** Wearing gloves, gently squeeze the excess soda ash solution from the ribbon without disturbing the clothespins.

**6.** Gently submerge the ribbon into the dyebath. Allow to soak for at least 30 minutes and up to an hour. Remove the ribbon from the dye and gently squeeze to remove any excess **(C)**, remembering to wear your gloves. (For more saturated color and sharper lines in the final pattern, wrap the ribbon in plastic and allow to cure for 24 hours before proceeding to step 7.)

**7.** With the clothespins still on the ribbon, rinse with cold water until the water runs clear. After rinsing out the excess dye, put the ribbon in a plastic container of water and add a capful of PTD. Swish the ribbon gently to clean **(D)**. Remove the clothespins and rinse with warm water until the water runs clear.

**8.** Gently roll up the ribbon in a clean rag or towel and press to remove excess water. Hang to dry and use an iron on the silk setting to press flat before using.

## TIP

To keep the patterns well defined and the whites very white in these ribbons, I chose to leave the clothespins on until the final rinse. You could also remove them after they emerge from the dyebath for softer patterns.

# Sunshine Play Tent

*This bright yellow play tent will be a favorite nook for your little ones for years to come. It is a perfect hideaway for toddlers and big kids alike, and it is pretty enough to be kept up all the time. A simple Internet search offered countless tent options. I found this one with pretty poles, little windows, and a handy pocket; most important, it was 100% cotton canvas.*

## SUPPLIES

Dyer's Kit (see page 20), including one wide 5-gallon (19 L) plastic container for dyeing and one 5-gallon (19 L) plastic container for curing

100% cotton canvas play tent, approximately 43 × 60" (107.5 × 150 cm)

4 gallons (15.4 L) of warm water

4 cups (1 kg) of soda ash

4 cups (1 kg) of dyer's salt

Fiber-reactive dye in yellow (I used Dharma Fiber Reactive Dye in Marigold)

## DYER'S NOTES

In this project, you might notice that the canvas tent is not being submerged in a soda ash soak. To avoid having a very heavy and messy presoaked tent, I added the soda ash directly to the dyebath. This will also wick dye up into the dry cloth, allowing a small amount of dye to seep into the area that is wound with twine. This creates a subtle ombré effect. Remember that once soda ash has been added to the dyebath, it will begin to lose strength immediately, so for the most saturated colors, have your tent bound and ready to go before you mix up the dyebath.

LEVEL:

SKILLS LEARNED:
Tub dyeing, dyeing solid colors, working large scale

FIBER:
Cellulose
(cotton)

DYE:
Fiber-reactive dye

## DIRECTIONS

**1.** Scour (see page 26) and dry the tent.

**2.** Spread out the tent on a large flat surface such a tabletop or floor and try to line up all the seams so it is flat. Find a spot on the tent about two-thirds of the way up from the bottom and bind it with a large rubber band. Add a second rubber band about 10" (25 cm) away. Wind the cotton twine tightly between the rubber bands **(A)**.

**3.** Prepare the dyebath: In the 5-gallon (19 L) plastic container, add 4 gallons (15.4 L) of warm tap water, 4 cups (1 kg) of soda ash and 4 cups (1 kg) of dyer's salt. Stir with a long spoon or stir stick until the salt and soda ash are fully dissolved. Put on your safety gear and make a slurry (see page 19) with 4 rounded teaspoons (19 g) of dye into 1 cup (240 ml) of warm water and add it to the container. Stir until the dye is completely dissolved.

**4.** Place only the top of the dry play tent (see Dyer's Notes on page 73) into the dyebath **(B)**, and use a stick or wooden spoon to submerge the top of the tent as necessary. Hold the top half of the canvas tent down in the dye until it begins to absorb the color. Set a timer for 1 hour and stir the tent frequently, yet gently in the dyebath to help the fiber dye more evenly.

**5.** After 1 hour, remove the top of the tent from the dyebath and wring any excess dye back into the bucket. Rotate the tent, placing the bottom half of the tent into the dyebath to soak. Make sure to have a clean towel or drop cloth on your work surface, as the top half of the canvas tent will drip dye onto it **(C)**. Submerge the canvas in the dyebath, set a timer for 1 hour, and stir frequently to help the tent dye more evenly as in step 4.

**6.** When the timer has gone off, wring as much excess dye into the container as possible—do your best! Note that when you are dyeing heavy fabrics and items with structure, it can often be difficult to wring out the dye. For this reason, with the twine still in place, put the tent into a large plastic bag and set it inside of a large plastic storage container to catch any excess dye. Leave to cure for 12 to 24 hours.

**7.** After the tent has cured for at least 12 hours, remove it from the plastic bag and unwind the resists **(D)**. Discard the used twine and rubber bands.

**8.** Wring out as much excess dye as possible before placing the tent in the washing machine and wash with hot water and PTD (see page 24). Machine-dry.

**9.** Use a hot iron on the cotton setting to remove any unwanted wrinkles from the tent before setting it up.

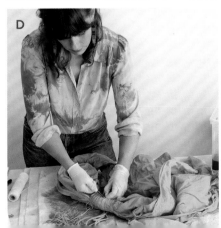

# Indigo Stripe Hammock

*This indigo-dyed hammock makes a perfect, cozy spot to rest and relax outside. I love the way this graphic indigo pattern looks totally at home in nature. This piece uses simple binding and several trips into the indigo vat to achieve the dark indigo color and contrasting organic white stripes.*

## SUPPLIES

Dyer's Kit (see page 20), including large rubber bands and a 5-gallon (19 L) bucket

100% cotton canvas hammock

5 large zip ties

Indigo kit (see Resources, page 158) or indigo vat (see page 30)

5-gallon (19 L) container of clean water

| LEVEL: | SKILLS LEARNED: | FIBER: | DYE: |
|---|---|---|---|
| ●●○○ | Tub dyeing, folding, adding resists, dyeing with indigo, working large scale | Cellulose (cotton) | Indigo |

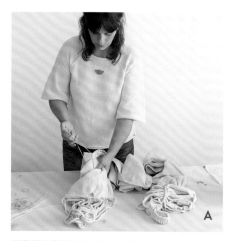

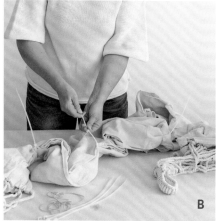

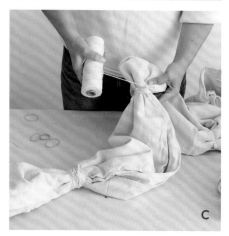

## DIRECTIONS

**1.** Scour the hammock (see page 26) to remove any starches or sizing from the item and dry. Lay the hammock out onto a clean surface and flatten out as many wrinkles as possible.

**2.** Accordion-fold the canvas width into 6" (15 cm) folds. When the entire hammock is folded, secure the folds in place near the ends with rubber bands so the hammock does not unravel while you work **( A )**.

**3.** Starting in the middle of the hammock, secure a plastic zip tie around the bulk of fabric and pull it as tightly as possible. Repeat with another zip tie at each end of the hammock, about 6" (15 cm) from the end, and then place another zip tie between the middle tie and the ties on either end. The hammock should be tied tightly with zip ties in five places **( B )**.

**4.** With the zip ties still in place, clip the long plastic ends off the ties and discard. Wrap cotton twine as tightly as possible around the areas that are secured with the zip ties. Cover and wrap an area that is at least 2" (5 cm) long, and secure the ends before moving on the next area to wrap **( C )**. After all of the zip ties have been tightly wrapped with string, place the hammock in a 5-gallon (19 L) bucket or container of clean water until fully soaked, at least 45 minutes.

**5.** Wring out any excess water. Wearing heavy gloves, place the hammock in the indigo vat **( D )** and hold it down until all the air bubbles are released and the hammock is submerged under the dyebath. If possible, do not allow any one part of the hammock to be exposed to the air while in the dye vat. This will cause the exposed part of the cotton to oxidize and turn a darker color of indigo, potentially causing dark and uneven spots on your project. Set a timer for 45 minutes and stir and turn the hammock frequently to help it dye evenly.

**6.** After the hammock has had time to absorb the indigo and the entire piece is a bright lime green, remove it from the indigo bath and wring it gently over the bucket to remove excess dye. Let the hammock rest, still tied, until the indigo is oxidized and the canvas is a deep indigo blue **( E )**. Repeat this process several times—the more repetitions, the darker the final shade of indigo will be.

**7.** When you have reached the desired shade, remove the twine and the zip ties and discard **(F)**. Unfold the hammock and allow to oxidize while fully open.

**8.** Rinse with cool water to removed unwanted dye (or do a short cold water cycle in your washing machine) and then wash with hot water and a PTD. Machine- or air-dry.

# FOR YOU

# Sunrise Blouse

*The ethereal patterns and surprising color combinations created by the ice-dyeing process used for this blouse are punctuated with little pops of bright citrus yellow. This V-neck blouse is super wearable and the hand-dyed decoration makes it memorable, as well. It will quickly become one of your go-to garments. Although rayon dyes like a dream, this technique can also be used with an all-cotton T-shirt.*

## SUPPLIES

Dyer's Kit (see page 20 and Dyer's Notes below for size of container needed)

100% rayon blouse

Soda ash soak (see page 27)

Cooling rack or similar wire rack

1 bag of ice (I used a 7-pound [3.2 kg] bag)

Fiber-reactive dye in gray and yellow (I used Dharma Fiber Reactive Dye in Mist Gray and Procion MX in Lemon Yellow)

## DYER'S NOTES

I purchased my wire rack and container at the same time to make sure they fit together and would not buckle under the weight of the ice used in this project. The container needs to be tall enough to catch all the melted ice and dye as it drips through the fabric. You can use the container for other dye projects, but the rack should not be used again for cooking or baking.

| LEVEL: | SKILLS LEARNED: | FIBER: | DYE: |
|---|---|---|---|
| ● ○ ○ ○ | Ice dyeing, color mixing | Cellulose (rayon) | Fiber-reactive dye |

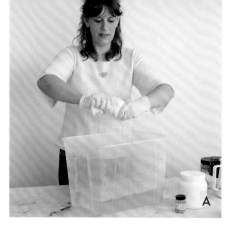

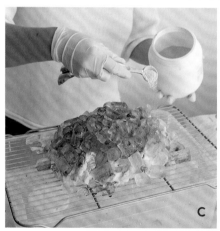

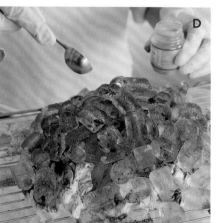

## DIRECTIONS

**1.** Scour the blouse (see page 26).

**2.** Place the blouse in the prepared soda ash soak. While the shirt is soaking, lay out a drop cloth to protect the dyeing surface, if needed. Place the wire rack on top of the plastic storage container and make sure that it is a good fit.

**3.** When the shirt is fully soaked, remove it from the soda ash bath and wring as much excess liquid back into the bucket as possible **(A)**.

**4.** Wearing clean gloves, fold the shirt in half lengthwise and gently crinkle into a compact shape **(B)**. (This is the Scrunch pattern on page 38.) Place the shirt on the rack and then cover the shirt in a layer of ice.

**5.** With your safety gear on, sprinkle the gray dye over the ice, covering the ice with a thin layer of dye **(C)**.

**6.** Using a clean spoon, scoop out about ⅛ rounded teaspoon (.5 g) of yellow dye and add tiny amounts to the ice, sprinkling it over the shirt **(D)**. Caution: A little bit of yellow goes a long way! The areas of yellow on the ice should be about the size of dimes after they start to dissolve. Add more yellow slowly, if needed.

**7.** Allow the ice to melt completely before removing the blouse, several hours to overnight. Discard the melted ice and dye down the sink or outside, and wash and dry the wire rack and container so they are clean when you want to use them again.

**8.** Rinse the blouse with cool running water and then hand-wash in warm water, using about 1 tablespoon (15 ml) of a PTD (see page 24). Rinse until the water runs clear, gently wring out the excess water, and hang or lay flat to dry. Press out any wrinkles with a steam iron set to "rayon."

# Tie-Dye Swimsuit

*I love the look of tie-dye at the beach. In this project, major style is added to a simple one-piece suit. I took my cue for the diagonal stripe design from the one-shoulder silhouette, but feel free to try other folding techniques. Learning to use acid dyes and dyes for polyester will open up an entire world of new items to dye—workout clothes, swimwear, even wigs and synthetic flowers can be dyed by hand.*

## SUPPLIES

Dyer's Kit (see page 20), including a wide 5-gallon (19 L) plastic container

White swimsuit in a synthetic blend (see Dyer's Notes below)

Small container of water

1 gallon (3.8 L) of boiling water

Acid dye in coral (I used Jacquard Acid Dye in Coral)

¼ cup (60 ml) of white vinegar

## DYER'S NOTES

Be sure to check the fiber content of your swimsuit before you begin this project. The suit I used is a blend of natural and synthetic fibers (modal, which is derived from rayon, and nylon), but if the suit you want to use is 100% polyester, you will need to use a product such as Jacquard's iDye Poly, which is specially formulated to work on tough-to-dye polyester. If you're dyeing a polyester suit, consult the instructions on the back of the dye instead of using the directions for this project.

| LEVEL: | SKILLS LEARNED: | FIBER: | DYE: |
|---|---|---|---|
| ● ● ○ ○ | Tub dyeing, folding, adding resists, dyeing with acid dye | Synthetic (modal and nylon blend) | Acid dye |

## DIRECTIONS

**1.** If the bodice of the swimsuit has removable cups, remove them and set them aside. Scour the suit by hand-washing with a capful of PTD (see page 24); hang to dry.

**2.** Lay the swimsuit flat on your work surface. Starting at the top of the suit, accordion-fold it at a 45-degree angle all the way down the length of the suit (**A**); this folding technique is a variation of the Accordion Fold pattern (see page 37). Note: When dyeing any swimsuit, pay special attention to the chest and crotch area. Make sure that those areas are folded and bound as evenly as the rest of the swimsuit so there are no awkward areas of solid color that may be unflattering.

**3.** When the suit has been folded all the way, hold it in place by securing it with rubber bands at both ends and in the middle. Slip one end of cotton twine under the rubber band to keep it in place (**B**) and tightly bind the entire length of the suit with twine; secure the end so it will not unravel. Soak the swimsuit in plain water while you prepare the dyebath.

**4.** Add the boiling water to the plastic container. Stir in 2 level teaspoons (9.5 g) of dye and mix until all the dye is dissolved. Add the white vinegar (**C**). Wring out the swimsuit and place it in the dyebath. Set a timer for 40 minutes and let the suit soak, stirring occasionally.

## DYER'S NOTES

When working with acid dyes, you typically simmer the items in the dyebath for a period of time. Because I did not want to lose any of the elasticity or structure of the swimsuit, I allowed the garment to simply soak in the boiling water as the water cooled instead of keeping it at a constant heat. This technique worked well to preserve the important characteristics of the delicate garment.

**5.** When the timer goes off, take the suit out of the dyebath. Remove the resists (**D**). Rinse the suit in warm water until the water runs clear, then gently hand-wash with 1 tablespoon (15 ml) of PTD and hang to dry.

**6.** Replace the removable cups, if needed, and go enjoy a day at the beach!

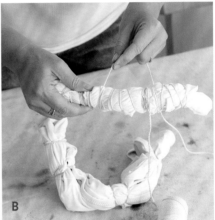

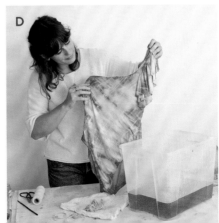

# Day-to-Night Dress

*This rayon dress, dyed in velvety black and crisp white, looks just right whether you are planning a day at home or a night out on the town. The rayon takes the black dye beautifully, creating very crisp and graphic patterns. For the blackest black, be sure to use hot water for the dye bath and cure the garment overnight.*

## SUPPLIES

Dyer's Kit (see page 20), including a 5-quart (4.7 L) or larger plastic container

White 100% rayon sleeveless dress

Soda ash soak (see page 27)

Fiber-reactive dye in black (I used Procion MX in Jet Black)

1 cup (280 g) of dyer's salt

1 quart (.9 L) boiling water

1 quart (.9 L) hot tap water

| LEVEL: | SKILLS LEARNED: | FIBER: | DYE: |
|---|---|---|---|
| ●●○○ | Tub dyeing, folding, adding resists, hot-water dyeing | Cellulose (rayon) | Fiber-reactive dye |

## DIRECTIONS

**1.** Scour the dress (see page 26), then iron or steam out any wrinkles.

**2.** Lay out the dress flat on a clean surface (a tabletop is ideal) and fold the dress in half lengthwise, aligning the side seams. Working from the top of the dress, begin accordion-folding it on about a 45-degree angle, keeping your folds even as you go **(A)**. Clip a clothespin every few inches (cm) down the length of the folded dress to keep the folds in place. This is like the Accordion Fold pattern (see page 37).

**3.** When the entire dress is folded, secure the folds by placing rubber bands every few inches (cm) down the length of the garment, then wrap the entire dress tightly with twine **(B)**. Note: The more tightly you wrap the dress, the less black there will be in the finished pattern.

**4.** Place the dress in the prepared soda ash soak and leave it until it is fully saturated, at least 30 minutes and up to several hours.

**5.** When the dress is soaked through and ready for dyeing, prepare the dye. (Remember to wear your safety gear when working with powdered dye.) Black dyes work best when they are used with very hot water. For example, I dyed this dress in 2 quarts (1.9 L) of water, which consisted of 1 quart (.9 L) of the hottest tap water possible and 1 quart (.9 L) of boiling water **(C)**. Consult the instructions on the back of the package of black dye to see what ratio they recommend for the blackest black, but as a general rule of thumb, it is twice the amount of dye you would normally use for any other color. To obtain the color you see in this project, use 4 rounded teaspoons (14 g) of black dye in 2 quarts (1.9 L) of almost boiling water.

Add 1 cup (280 g) of dyer's salt and stir well until there is no undissolved dye.

**6.** Wring out as much excess liquid from the dress as possible and place it in the dyebath—be careful not to burn your fingers! Remember that you're working with hot water for this project.

**7.** Submerge the dress in the dye **(D)** and allow it to soak for at least 2 hours and up to 4 hours, stirring occasionally.

**8.** Wring out the excess dye and place the dress in a plastic bag to cure for 24 hours. It is important to allow the dress to cure for the full amount of time to achieve the richest, most velvety black. After 24 hours, rinse the dress well under cold running water and then unwrap and discard the resists.

**9.** Machine-wash the dress in hot water with a PTD (see page 24). Machine-dry and use a hot iron on the steam setting to smooth out the wrinkles.

# Wooden Bead Necklace

*I really like to experiment with unconventional materials when I am in the dye studio, and this wooden bead necklace is no exception. The dye creates tiny bursts of bright color, and the result looks almost as if the beads have been marbled. A quick coat of matte finish spray will ensure that the beads do not transfer dye when the necklace is worn. This is a fun project to work on with kids.*

## SUPPLIES

Dyer's Kit (see page 20), including 1-pint (500 ml) glass canning jar

2 cups (480 ml) of warm water

3 level tablespoons (43 g) of soda ash

Approximately 10 wooden beads, each 1" (2.5 cm) in diameter

Fiber-reactive dye in magenta and cyan (I used Procion MX in Magenta and Turquoise)

Fine-tipped permanent marker (optional)

Chopstick (optional)

Matte finish spray

1 yard (.9 m) of leather cord (or as much as needed for desired length)

| LEVEL: | SKILLS LEARNED: | FIBER: | DYE: |
|---|---|---|---|
| ●○○○ | Mixing colors, working with unconventional materials, working small scale | Cellulose (wood) | Fiber-reactive dye |

## DIRECTIONS

**1.** In a glass jar (or other container that will not be used again for food), add the warm water and soda ash. Stir until all of the soda ash has dissolved. Add seven of the wooden beads to the mixture and let them soak for about 10 minutes **(A)**.

A

**2.** Sprinkle a tiny bit (⅛ rounded teaspoon [.5 g]) of cyan dye on top of the wooden beads. Using a spoon, gently stir and turn the beads to cover them more evenly with the dye. Next add a tiny sprinkle (⅛ rounded teaspoon [.5 g]) of magenta dye to the mix and stir **(B)**. The beads should have a marbled, watercolor look to the surface. Feel free to add more dye to the mixture until your desired color is achieved.

**3.** When you're happy with the color, remove the beads from the container. Under running water, rinse off any trace dye and then place the beads on paper towels to dry.

B

**4.** On the remaining three beads, make a decorative, graphic pattern with permanent marker. This is much easier to do if you secure each bead on the end of a chopstick while you make your patterns **(C)**. If you'd prefer, you can also dye all 10 beads instead.

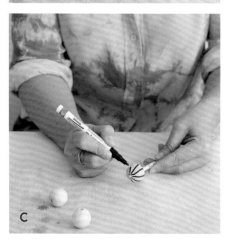

**5.** When the beads are completely dry—several hours or overnight—spray them with a light coat of matte finish spray following the manufacturer's instructions.

C

**6.** Cut a 30" (75 cm) length of natural leather cord and string the beads on it **(D)**. To finish the necklace, secure the cord with a simple square knot.

D

# Tropical Green Kaftan

*I love dyeing and wearing rayon gauze; the texture is light as air, it has a beautiful drape, and the textile takes color like a dream. The geometric pattern of this project combined with the deep green color makes for a stunning combination on this warm-weather piece. The kaftan requires a little bit of careful folding as well as the mixing of a custom color, but the results are well worth the effort.*

## SUPPLIES

Dyer's Kit (see page 20), including 20 to 25 clothespins and a wide 5-gallon (19 L) plastic container

100% rayon kaftan (you can also use a cotton, linen, or bamboo garment)

Soda ash soak (see page 27)

3 gallons (11.4 L) of very hot water

Fiber-reactive dye in black, cyan, and green (I used Procion MX in Jet Black and Turquoise, and Dharma Fiber Reactive Dye in Celadon)

4 cups (1 kg) of dyer's salt

| LEVEL: | SKILLS LEARNED: | FIBER: | DYE: |
|---|---|---|---|
| ● ● ○ ○ | Tub dyeing, folding, adding resists, mixing custom colors | Cellulose (rayon) | Fiber-reactive dye |

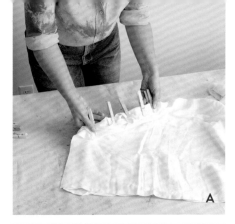

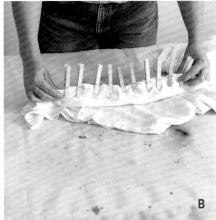

## DIRECTIONS

**1.** Scour the garment (see page 26). Prepare the soda ash soak. Iron or steam the kaftan to remove any wrinkles and lay it on a large, clean surface. Fold the garment in half lengthwise and smooth it flat.

**2.** Fold the kaftan back and forth in an accordion pattern along the diagonal (like the Accordion Fold pattern on page 37), following the angle of the V-neck of the garment. Secure the folds with clothespins as you go **(A)**. The bundle should be about 8 folds tall.

**3.** Once the folds are secured with clothespins, go back in and clamp more clothespins to the folded neckline until the length is covered and secure **(B)**. Soak the kaftan in the soda ash bath for at least 10 minutes while you prepare the dye.

**4.** Add 3 gallons (11.4 L) of very hot water to the 5-gallon (19 L) container. Note that hot water must be used to activate the black in this rich green custom color. Put on your mask and gloves and make a slurry (see page 19) consisting of the following:

• 3 level tablespoons (43 g) black
• 2 level tablespoons (28.5 g) cyan
• 5 rounded tablespoons (100 g) green

Add the slurry to the hot water, along with 4 cups (1 kg) of dyer's salt.

**5.** After the kaftan has soaked in the soda ash bath, squeeze out any excess liquid, being careful not to move the clothespins, and then add the garment to the dyebath **(C)**. With a stick or wooden spoon, gently stir the kaftan every 15 to 20 minutes to help ensure that the garment dyes evenly. Soak for a total of 2 to 4 hours, stirring frequently, depending on the depth of color that you want.

**6.** Remove the kaftan from the dyebath and squeeze out any excess. With the clothespins still in place, wrap the kaftan in a plastic bag and allow to cure for at least 12 hours, preferably overnight **(D)**.

**7.** After curing, remove the clothespins and rinse the garment in cold water until the water runs clear. Machine-wash in hot water with a PTD (see page 24) and then machine-dry. Use a hot iron on the steam setting to smooth out any wrinkles. After the first wash, machine-wash cold with like colors and machine-dry.

# Northern Lights Scarf

*The combination of ice dyeing and shibori folding on this silk chiffon scarf yields brilliant color and a kaleidoscope of unexpected organic patterns. The warm gray and pale pink dyes expand and break apart when they encounter the ice, melting into a beautiful blend of colors. Silk is warm in the winter and cool in the summer, and the oversize piece used in this project can also function as a sarong or light blanket, making it the ultimate accessory.*

## SUPPLIES

Dyer's Kit (see page 20 and Dyer's Notes below for size of container needed)

100% silk sarong, 43 × 75" (107.5 × 187.5 cm)

Soda ash soak (see page 27)

Cooling rack or similar wire rack

1 bag of ice (I used a 7-pound [3.2 kg] bag)

Fiber-reactive dye in gray and pink (I used Dharma Fiber Reactive Dye in Mist Gray and Light Pink)

## DYER'S NOTES

I purchased my wire rack and container at the same time to make sure they fit together and would not buckle under the weight of the ice used in this project. The container needs to be tall enough to catch all the melted ice and dye as it drips through the fabric. You can use the container for other dye projects, but the rack should not be used again for cooking or baking.

| LEVEL: | SKILLS LEARNED: | FIBER: | DYE: |
|--------|-----------------|--------|------|
| ●●○○ | Ice dyeing, folding | Protein (Silk) | Fiber-reactive dye |

## DIRECTIONS

**1.** Scour the scarf by hand-washing in room-temperature water with a scant capful of PTD (see page 24); hang and let dry.

**2.** Place the silk scarf into the prepared soda ash soak. Note that too much time in the soda ash bath can weaken the silk fibers, so soak the scarf only until fully saturated, about 10 minutes.

**3.** While the scarf is soaking, lay out a drop cloth to protect the dyeing surface. Place the rack on top of the container; make sure that it is sturdy and will not fall under the weight of the ice **(A)**.

**4.** When the scarf is saturated, put on clean, protective gloves, remove the scarf from the soda ash soak and wring as much excess liquid back into the container as possible.

**5.** Gently unwring the scarf and shake out the wrinkles. Fold the scarf in half lengthwise and then in half again, making a long accordion fold (see page 37). Lay the accordion-folded silk down on a clean work surface and fold over one corner of the silk to form a triangle (see the Itajime Triangle pattern on page 39). Continue to fold the silk into a stack of triangles **(B)**. Be patient when you're working with the wet silk, as it can be a little tricky—you can always shake out your folds and start over if you're not satisfied with the results.

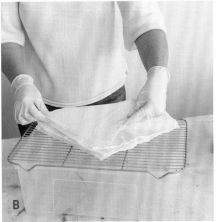

**6.** When the silk is folded, place it in the center of wire rack. Lift up the folds of silk to expose the bottom layer and add a mound of ice (about 1 cup [227 g]). Sprinkle 1 rounded teaspoon (5 g) of each of the dyes over the mound of ice **(C)**.

**7.** Repeat step 6 for each large fold in the stack until you have both ice and dye sandwiched between the layers of the folded silk. Pour the remaining ice over the scarf and arrange it so that there is little to no silk exposed. Sprinkle an additional 2 rounded teaspoons (9.5 g) of each dye over the mound of ice **(D)**.

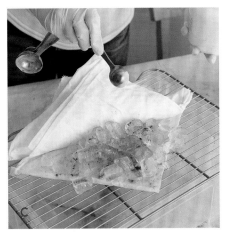

**8.** Allow the ice to melt completely before removing the silk, from several hours to overnight. Discard the water and dye down the sink or outside, and wash and dry the wire rack and container so they are clean when you want to use them again.

**9.** Be careful when you wash silk—exposure to extreme temperature changes can "shock" the protein fibers, causing them to lose some of their drape and softness. Be sure to use cool water that gradually changes to warm to rinse this piece. After rinsing, then hand-wash in warm water with about 1 tablespoon (15 ml) of PTD. Rinse until the water runs clear, gently wring out the excess water, and hang or lay flat to dry. Press out any wrinkles with an iron set to "silk."

# Super Bloom Robe

*This robe is one of my favorite pieces. I love how the garment is so elegant and so effortless at the same time, with a spiral pattern highlighting the back. The colors of the robe were inspired by the intense palette of the blooming desert. This pattern is one of my favorite ways to layer dye, because it results in beautiful depth and intriguing variation in the colors.*

## SUPPLIES

Dyer's Kit (see page 20), including two wide 5-gallon (19 L) plastic containers

100% rayon robe

Soda ash soak (see page 27)

6 gallons (22.8 L) of warm water

6 cups (1.7 kg) of dyer's salt

Fiber-reactive dye in magenta and light pink (I used Procion MX in Raspberry and Dharma Fiber Reactive Dye in Light Pink)

| LEVEL:<br>● ● ○ ○ | SKILLS LEARNED:<br>Tub dyeing, twisting, applying resists, layering colors | FIBER:<br>Cellulose (rayon) | DYE:<br>Fiber-reactive dye |
|---|---|---|---|

## DIRECTIONS

**1.** Scour the garment (see page 26). Remove the tie from the robe, scrunch the tie into a ball, secure with rubber bands, and set aside.

**2.** Lay the robe out flat on clean surface with the back of the robe facing up. Pinch a point on the upper right shoulder of the robe. Holding the fabric between your thumb and forefinger, twist the rayon clockwise so that the fabric forms a tight swirl **(A)** and secure loosely in place with a rubber band. (You'll be creating the variation of the Scrunch pattern mentioned on page 38. It can feel unruly when you start scrunching up the robe for this allover pattern, but just continue working the fabric into even crinkles and securing it in place. It is okay to start over as many times as you need to!)

**3.** Evenly scrunch the remaining fabric of the sleeves and the top half of the robe around the swirl you formed in step 2, forming a shape that looks like a fat disk of fabric. Secure with rubber bands **(B)**.

**4.** Rotate the robe and make another swirl pattern at the bottom hem on the front side of the robe **(C)** and scrunch the remaining fabric to incorporate it into the disk. Secure with more rubber bands, crinkling any loose fabric until the surface is uniform.

**5.** Using another rubber band or string, secure the belt to the robe so they stay together. (I have lost so many belts! One of my students suggested this perfect solution during a workshop.) Add the robe to the soda ash solution and let soak for at least 10 minutes.

**6.** Fill the container with 3 gallons (11.4 L) of warm water and add 3 cups (840 g) of dyer's salt. Make a slurry (see page 19) with 3 rounded teaspoons (14 g) of light pink dye in a glass jar and add it to the container. Remember to wear your safety gear while preparing the slurries in this step and in step 8.

**7.** Add the robe to the dyebath and allow to soak for 45 minutes to 1 hour (or longer for a stronger, brighter light pink).

**8.** While the robe is soaking in the first color, prepare the second dyebath in a separate container, again using 3 gallons (11.4 L) of warm water and 3 cups (840 g) of dyer's salt. Make another slurry with 4 rounded teaspoons (19 g) of magenta dye and add it to the bucket.

**9.** After the robe has reached the desired shade of pink, remove it from the dye and squeeze out any excess **(D)**. Hold the robe in both hands and twist the bundle, shifting it slightly to reveal undyed (white) areas. This subtle movement is what creates the final pattern—areas of pure light pink, pure magenta, and a mix of the two.

**10.** Place the robe and tie into the magenta dyebath and allow to soak for 45 minutes to 2 hours, depending on how dark you want your magenta shade to be. When you have reached the desired color, squeeze out as much excess dye as possible **(E)**. With the rubber bands still in place, wrap the robe and tie in a plastic bag to cure for 12 to 24 hours. I usually leave my pieces to cure overnight.

**11.** After the robe has cured, undo the rubber bands **(F)**. Rinse the robe and tie in cold water until the water runs clean and then machine-wash in hot water with a PTD (see page 24). Machine-dry and use a hot iron on the steam setting to smooth out any wrinkles. After the first wash, machine-wash cold with like colors and machine-dry.

# FOR YOUR HOME

# Stamped Table Linens

*I love working with hand-carved wooden stamps from India. Traditionally used for hand printing fabric with plant-based dyes, the fine lines of the teak stamps transfer well onto these linens. The rich, sunny shade of yellow makes for a stylish table setting. The stamping technique used in this project would also be really beautiful for a more advanced bedding project or for a lovely set of hand-stamped curtains.*

## SUPPLIES

Dyer's Kit (see page 20), including a roll of paper towels

Cotton napkins and/or placemats (linen would also work well), as many as desired

Soda ash soak (see page 27)

Fiber-reactive dye in yellow (I used Dharma Fiber Reactive Dye in Marigold)

Sodium alginate

A piece of Plexiglas or a ceramic plate larger than the stamp

Hand-carved stamp

## TIP

You can find hand-carved stamps from India online, in craft or import stores, or even thrift shops. If you make sure to clean and dry your stamps after each use, these beautiful handmade objects will last you a lifetime. If you are interested in learning how to carve your own stamps for this project, my first book, *Stamp Stencil Paint: Making Extraordinary Patterned Projects by Hand*, will take you through the process step by step.

| LEVEL: | SKILLS LEARNED: | FIBER: | DYE: |
|---|---|---|---|
| ●○○○ | Hand stamping, direct dye application, thickening a dye | Cellulose (cotton) | Fiber-reactive dye |

## DIRECTIONS

**1.** Scour the table linens (see page 26).

**2.** Add the napkins and placemats to the prepared soda ash soak and leave until fully saturated, at least 15 to 20 minutes. When they are soaked through, wring the excess liquid back into the bucket and let the napkins air-dry. (Stamping on the napkins when they are dry will keep the dye from bleeding.)

**3.** In a pint-size (500 ml) glass canning jar or plastic container, make a slurry (see page 19) using 3 rounded teaspoons (14 g) of yellow dye. Stir until all the lumps of dry dye have dissolved and then sprinkle with ¼ teaspoon (1.2 g) of sodium alginate. Wait at least 10 minutes before adding more sodium alginate, as it will continue to thicken the dye while it sits. The dye is ready for stamping when it is slightly thickened, with the viscosity of melted butter. Stir with a utensil until smooth **(A)**. Note: Adding a little bit of sodium alginate to thicken the dye used in this project helps in a couple of important ways—it will help make crisper prints with the stamps and also keep the stamped dye from bleeding in the wash.

**4.** If you haven't done so already, cover your work surface with several lay-ers of newsprint to keep it protected. Stack three paper towels and fold the stack in half. Place the folded paper towels onto the Plexiglas sheet or ceramic plate—if using a plate, make sure that the entire stamp will fit within the flat area of the plate. Otherwise, it will not print evenly.

**5.** Slowly pour a small amount of dye onto the center of the paper towels and allow it to absorb, adding little more each time until the dye has fully saturated an area the size of the stamp **(B)**.

**6.** Wearing gloves, if you prefer, place the stamp facedown into the dye stamp "pad" that you just made and dab it up and down on the surface of the paper towel. Use a light hand so that the dye does not pool in the carved areas of the stamp, which will bleed when the stamp touches the surface of the napkin. You may want to test the coverage of the dye on the stamp by stamping onto a damp paper towel **(C)**. Discard the towel after testing.

**7.** Cover the surface of the stamp with dye once more and place it onto the top left-hand corner of the napkin. Press down evenly on the entire back of the stamp with the heel of your hand and lift away. Repeat this process, stamping from left to right, to create a row along the entire top of the napkin, leaving about 1" (2.5 cm) in between stamps. If desired, rotate the stamp 180 degrees every other print, as shown (see next step).

**8.** Repeat step 7 on the second row, staggering the first print so that it stamps in between the prints on the top row, creating a tile pattern. Continue to stamp the entire surface of the napkin, staggering every other row, if desired, **(D)**. Mix another batch of thickened dye according to instructions in step 3 and add to the "stamp pad" as needed to stamp all the linens you would like. (Do you see the arrow on the stamp? This shows the correct orientation of the design when you're stamping, so it's a helpful way to make sure you're printing the pattern as you had intended.)

**9.** Allow the printed napkins and placemats to dry completely before washing. Under cold running water, rinse the printed surface of the linens gently to remove any excess dye from the surface of the fabric. When the water runs clear, wash the linens in your washing machine in hot water with a PTD (see page 24) and machine-dry. Use a hot iron on the cotton setting to smooth out any wrinkles.

D

# Storm Clouds Duvet Set

*This bedding set is so simple to dye yet makes a beautiful, stylish statement for your bedroom. The rich and complex pattern is created from some easy folding and just a few rubber bands. The subtle cool gray hue works for any season; this color looks great mixed and matched with other neutral colors and patterns, so it's a welcome addition to your linen closet.*

## SUPPLIES

Dyer's Kit (see page 20), including a wide 5-gallon (19 L) plastic container

100% cotton duvet cover and pillowcase set (100% linen bedding will dye equally well), any size

Soda ash soak (see page 27)

Fiber-reactive dye in gray and light purple (I used Procion MX Neutral Gray and Lilac)

3½ gallons (13.3 L) of warm water

3 cups (840 g) of dyer's salt

| LEVEL: | SKILLS LEARNED: | FIBER: | DYE: |
|---|---|---|---|
| ●○○○ | Tub dyeing, folding, adding resists, mixing custom colors, working large scale | Cellulose (cotton) | Fiber-reactive dye |

## DIRECTIONS

**1.** Scour the linens (see page 26). Start the folding process with the pillowcases—place them on a clean surface such as a tabletop or floor and smooth away any wrinkles. Accordion-fold (see page 37) each pillowcase widthwise into a stack of 4 equal-size folds, roughly 4" (10 cm) wide. Starting at the bottom corner, fold the fabric into triangles, forming a triangular stack **(A)**. This folding action is essentially the Itajime Triangle pattern (see page 39), but no clamps will be used.

**2.** Secure each corner of the triangle with tightly wound rubber bands **(B)**. Set aside and repeat with the second pillowcase.

**3.** Unfold the duvet cover, lay it flat, and smooth out any wrinkles. Fold the duvet cover lengthwise into an accordion—depending on the size of the duvet, the number of the folds will vary. For the queen-size duvet used here, the accordion of fabric was 6 folds high and about 10" (25 cm) wide. After the duvet has been folded into a long strip, fold it into triangles like the pillowcases **(C)**.

**4.** Secure the corners of the triangle with tightly wound rubber bands, placing them about 4" (10 cm) in from the end of the triangle. After all the bedding is securely bound, soak it in the prepared soda ash solution for at least 1 hour, until the cotton is fully saturated.

**5.** While the bedding is soaking, prepare the dyebath. Add 3½ gallons (13.3 L) of warm water to the 5-gallon (15.4 L) container. In a small pint glass jar, make a slurry (see page 19) of 2 rounded teaspoons (9.5 g) of gray dye, 1 level teaspoon (4.5 g) of light purple dye, and ½ cup (120 ml) of warm water **(D)**, being sure to wear your mask. Mix with a plastic spoon or chopstick until here are no more lumps of dry dye and the mixture is smooth.

**6.** Add the dye slurry to the container and stir. Add 3 cups (840 g) of dyer's salt and stir until fully dissolved. Test the tone of the color with a scrap of cotton or linen, and make any adjustments to the color before dyeing the bedding itself **(E)**.

**7.** Squeeze the excess soda ash solution from the linens and submerge them in the dyebath. Allow them to soak for 2 to 4 hours—soak for the full 4 hours for a darker, more saturated color—stirring and turning the bedding occasionally.

**8.** After the bedding has been dyed to your satisfaction, squeeze out all excess dye and wrap the bedding tightly in a plastic trash bag. Let the bedding cure for a full 24 hours for the most intense color and sharpest patterns—for this combination of color and pattern, the curing time is very important.

**9.** After 24 hours, remove and discard the rubber bands from the pillowcases and duvet cover **(F)**, unfold the bedding, and wash in hot water in the washing machine with a PTD (see page 24). Machine-dry and iron if needed.

### DYER'S NOTES

If you are looking for a subtler color for your duvet, omit the purple dye in the color recipe in step 5 and replace it with 1 additional rounded teaspoon (4.5 g) of gray dye.

D

E

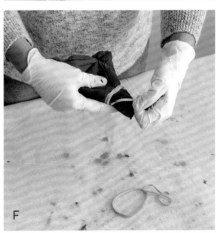

F

# Sea Glass Bath Towels

*These lovely bath towels are so simple to dye and will add beautiful color and pattern to your bathroom or a beach trip. The key to getting sharp pattern lines in the thirsty terry cloth is allowing them to cure a full twenty-four hours after being dyed. This is the perfect project to add new life to white towels that have seen better days—you can do them all in the same pattern or mix and match for a more bohemian vibe.*

## SUPPLIES

Dyer's Kit (page 20), including a wide 5-gallon (19 L) plastic container

100% cotton terry cloth towels (I dyed 4 for this project)

Soda ash soak (page 27)

Fiber-reactive dye in sea green (I used Dharma Fiber Reactive Dye in Celadon)

4 gallons (15.4 L) of warm water

| LEVEL: | SKILLS LEARNED: | FIBER: | DYE: |
|---|---|---|---|
| ●○○○ | Folding, adding resists, working large scale | Cellulose (cotton) | Fiber-reactive dye |

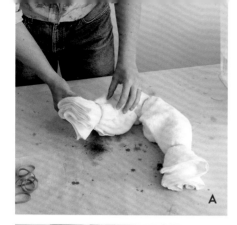

## DIRECTIONS

**1.** Scour the towels (see page 26).

**2.** Lay a towel out on a clean surface such as a table or the floor and smooth it flat. Accordion-fold the towel widthwise until it is folded into a stack (similar to the Accordion Fold pattern on page 37). Bind a rubber band as tightly as possible at the end of the towel, about 4" (10 cm) in from the end. Repeat at the other end of the towel. Place another rubber band in the middle of the towel, between the rubber bands already placed at the ends of the towel **(A)**. Repeat to bind all the towels you wish to dye.

**3.** Place the bound towels in the prepared soda ash bath and leave until they are fully saturated and have sunk to the bottom of the bucket, between 10 and 45 minutes.

**4.** While the towels are soaking, prepare the dyebath. Wear your safety gear and make a slurry (see page 19) of ½ cup (120 ml) water and 4 rounded teaspoons (19 g) of sea green dye. Add the dye slurry to the warm water in the container and stir to make sure that all of the dye is fully dissolved **(B)**.

**5.** Submerge all of the bound towels in the dyebath. Set a timer for 1 hour and, after it goes off, check the color **(C)**. For a deeper shade, let the towels soak in the dyebath longer—up to 4 hours.

**6.** When the desired color is achieved, squeeze out as much dye as possible **(D)** and store the towels in a plastic bag to cure for a full 24 hours before washing.

**7.** Rinse the towels with cool water until the water runs clear. Wash in the washing machine on hot water with a PTD (see page 24). After the first wash, machine-wash and dry with like colors.

# Elegant Linen Tablecloth

*The warm colorway used in this linen tablecloth—a combination of soft pink and tan—will complement any feast you lay on the table. In the summer, you could dress it casually with simple wildflowers, and in the winter, you can add jewel tones for a laid-back holiday setting. This project would be lovely with matching napkins or mix it up with the Stamped Table Linens on page 107. I chose to dye a long, rectangular tablecloth, but this pattern can be adapted to work on a square tablecloth as well.*

## SUPPLIES

Dyer's Kit (see page 20), including a wide 5-gallon (19 L) plastic container

100% linen tablecloth (100% cotton tablecloth would dye equally well),
57 × 95" (145 × 237.5 cm)

Large C-clamp, at least 6" (15 cm)

2 wooden or plastic boards for clamping, 4" (10 cm) circle or square
(large canning jar lids will work well also)

Soda ash soak (see page 27)

Fiber-reactive dye in pink and tan (I used Dharma Fiber Reactive Dye in Light
Pink and Ecru)

6 gallons (22.8 L) of water

6 cups (1.6 kg) of dyer's salt

| LEVEL: | SKILLS LEARNED: | FIBER: | DYE: |
|---|---|---|---|
| ●●○○ | Tub dyeing, folding, clamping, layering color, working large scale | Cellulose (linen) | Fiber-reactive dye |

## DIRECTIONS

**1.** Scour the tablecloth (see page 26).

**2.** Iron the tablecloth so that there are no wrinkles. Lay the tablecloth flat on a large, clean table or floor and fold it in half lengthwise, smooth any wrinkles, then accordion-fold until the tablecloth is approximately 7 to 8" (17.5 to 20 cm) wide.

**3.** Fold up a triangle at one end **(A)** and fold until the entire tablecloth is folded into a neat stack **(B)**. This is the Itajime Triangle pattern (see page 39). Temporarily secure in place with a rubber band (or have someone help you hold it in place).

**4.** Place the resists on the folded fabric, one on either side, centering them in the middle of the stacked triangle. Place the C-clamp over the disks and screw down to sandwich the resists around the fabric **(C)**. Place the clamped fabric in the prepared soda ash soak for at least 20 minutes.

**5.** Don your safety gear and prepare your first dyebath while the linen is soaking. In the large container, add 3 gallons (11.4 L) of water. Make a slurry (see page 19) with 2 rounded teaspoons (9.5 g) of pink dye and add it to the tub. Add 3 cups (840 g) of dyer's salt and stir well. Submerge the presoaked tablecloth in the dyebath and soak for 45 minutes to 1 hour—soak longer for a deeper pink color.

**6.** Remove the tablecloth from the first dyebath and set it aside on a clean surface to rest while you prepare the second dye color. Do not unclamp.

**7.** Discard the pink dyebath and mix the second color. (You could also save the pink dyebath for another project, as it will be good for about 2 hours after first use.) Add 3 rounded teaspoons (14 g) of tan dye to 3 gallons (11.4 L) of tap water, along with 3 cups (840 g) of dyer's salt. Place the tablecloth in the dyebath **(D)** and allow to soak for at least 2 hours.

**8.** When you remove the tablecloth from the second dyebath, keep it clamped and wrap the project in a plastic bag. Allow it to cure at room temperature for up to 24 hours. This will ensure the deepest color and crispest lines.

**9.** After the tablecloth has cured, unclamp the cloth and rinse it in cold water to stop the dye reaction. When the water runs clear, machine-wash the tablecloth in hot water with a PTD (see page 24), and machine- or line-dry. Use an iron with steam on the linen setting to ease out any wrinkles.

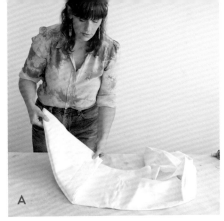

# Shibori Pendant Lamp

*Nothing pulls a room together better than a designer light fixture, and this showstopping lamp is no exception. The shade on this large drum pendant is a stylish and unexpected way to use hand-dyed patterns in the home. I used a fine, slightly transparent cotton dyed in indigo for this statement piece, which allows the light to shine through and lets the crisp shibori pattern take center stage.*

## SUPPLIES

Dyer's Kit (see page 20), including a 5-gallon (19 L) bucket

Thin quilter's cotton or cotton voile (see Fabric Notes to determine the amount needed)

2 wooden or plastic blocks, 4" (10 cm) square

C-clamp or large spring clamp

5-gallon (19 L) container of clean water

Indigo kit (see Resources, page 158) or indigo vat (see page 30)

Pendant lamp with white shade (the one shown here is 16 × 28" [40 × 70 cm])

Transparent fabric glue (I prefer Fabri-Tac Permanent Adhesive)

Lint roller (optional)

## FABRIC NOTES

The amount of fabric you need depends on the size of the lampshade you will be covering. Measure the height and the circumference of the lampshade and buy the amount of fabric that equals that measurement, plus at least ¼ yard (9"/22.5 cm) extra to accommodate shrinkage during the dyeing process.

| LEVEL: | SKILLS LEARNED: | FIBER: | DYE: |
|---|---|---|---|
| ●●○○ | Tub dyeing, folding, clamping, dyeing with indigo | Cellulose (cotton) | Indigo |

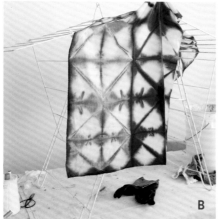

## DIRECTIONS

**1.** Scour the fabric (see page 26).

**2.** On a flat, clean surface such as a tabletop or the floor, accordion-fold the fabric lengthwise into 5" (12.5 cm) pleats. Fold up a triangle at one end and continue until the entire strip is folded into a neat stack. This is the Itajime Triangle pattern (see page 39).

**3.** After folding, place the blocks on either side of the folded triangle, at the center, and tightly clamp into place **(A)**. Soak the clamped fabric in the clean water until fully saturated, at least 15 minutes.

**4.** When the fabric is fully soaked, squeeze out excess water and submerge the clamped fabric in the indigo vat. Allow to soak for 25 to 40 minutes. Remove the clamped fabric from the indigo bath and squeeze the excess dye back into the vat without removing the clamps. Allow to oxidize (see page 33) while still folded and then place the bundle back into the indigo vat for another 30 to 45 minutes.

**5.** After the second time in the dyebath, squeeze out the extra dye and unfold. Allow the fabric to oxidize on a drying rack or clothesline **(B)**.

**6.** When the indigo is fully oxidized, rinse it until the water runs clear and then hand-wash with a small amount of PTD; consult the label for instructions, but a capful or so is probably enough. Hang to dry.

**7.** Press out any wrinkles with your iron on the cotton setting **(C)**.

**8.** Trim the fabric to the appropriate length and width to cover the lamp shade, including an additional 1" (2.5 cm) border on all sides. Carefully fold over the fabric, add some glue, and finger-press in place. Go around all the edges, gluing and pressing as you go **(D)**, until all of the fabric is secured to the lampshade. Fold over the edges and glue to cover the "seam" at the starting point.

**9.** If necessary, clean using a lint roller.

# Points of Light Pillows

*The patterns on these pillows are inspired by Japanese sashiko. Sashiko is a hand-stitching technique for mending and reinforcing garments using beautiful, intricate stitches. Instead of stitches, however, the reverse patterns in this project are made with bleach paste applied through stencils; the pillow covers are hand dyed first. I am enamored with how this process embeds the intricate patterns into the fiber and adds subtle color and texture variations to the final pieces. I have offered two stencil templates on page 157, but feel free to experiment with your own designs and stencil ideas.*

## SUPPLIES

Dyer's Kit (see page 20), including two wide 5-gallon (19 L) plastic containers and one 5-gallon (19 L) bucket

100% linen pillow covers in your choice of sizes (I used 20 × 20" [50 × 50 cm], 26 × 26" [65 × 65 cm], and 16 × 24" [40 × 60 cm] covers, for a total of 6 pillows)

Soda ash soak (see page 27)

Indigo kit (see Resources, page 158) or indigo vat (see page 30)

4 gallons (15.4 L) warm water

Fiber-reactive dye in orange and warm gray (I used Dharma Fiber Reactive Dye in Terracotta and Shitake Mushroom)

4 cups (1 kg) of dyer's salt

One 8½ × 11" (21.5 × 28 cm) piece of plastic stencil film or sheet of medium-weight Mylar for each template

Templates (see page 157)

Fine-tipped permanent marker

*continued*

| LEVEL: | SKILLS LEARNED: | FIBER: | DYE: |
|---|---|---|---|
|  | Tub dyeing, dyeing solid colors, dyeing with indigo, cutting stencils, working with bleach paste | Cellulose (linen) | Fiber-reactive dye and indigo |

Self-healing cutting mat

Japanese screw punch tool (also known as a bookbinding hole punch or drill)

Hammer or mallet

Bleach

Bleach-thickening paste

Small stencil brush

Pillow inserts in sizes to fit your pillow covers

## DIRECTIONS

**1.** Scour all the pillow covers you wish to dye (see page 26).

**2.** Place the pillow covers being dyed in fiber reactive dye in the prepared soda ash soak until fully saturated, at least 30 minutes. The covers being dyed in indigo do not need to be soaked in the soda ash bath.

**3.** While the pillow covers are soaking, prepare the dyebaths, wearing your safety gear. In a 5-gallon (19 L) bucket, set up an indigo vat or follow the directions in your indigo kit. To each of the remaining 5-gallon (19 L) containers, add approximately 2 gallons (7.6 L) of warm tap water.

**4.** Add a slurry (see page 19) of 3 rounded teaspoons (14 g) of orange dye to one of the containers of water; to the other, add a slurry of 3 rounded teaspoons (14 g) of gray dye **(A)**. Add 2 cups (560 g) of dyer's salt to each container and stir each bath well until all of the dye has dissolved.

**5.** Remove the presoaked pillow covers from the soda ash, wring as much excess liquid as possible back into the container, and place the desired quantity of pillow covers into the dyebaths of your choice. I dyed two pillow covers in each of the three colors. Set a timer for 45 minutes. Stir each fiber-reactive dye vat frequently to help ensure that the pillow covers dye evenly.

**6.** When the timer goes off, check the pillow covers and remove or allow them soak longer for bolder, more saturated colors **(B)**. For the pillow covers in the indigo vat, soak them, remove them from the vat, let them oxidize, and then repeat for darker indigo tones. If you prefer lighter tones, allow them to sit in the bath only until fully saturated and remove right away—about 10 minutes. However, the 45 minutes recommended for the fiber-reactive dyes will result in an even, medium-dark tone.

**TIP**

For a different look, try layering bleach paste patterns over indigo-dyed patterns. Consult Basic Pattern Resists (see page 34) for more ideas, and read more about indigo on page 30.

**7.** When the pillow covers being dyed in the fiber-reactive baths have reached the desired color, remove them from the dyebath, wring out any excess dye, and place each in its own clean plastic bag to cure for 12 to 24 hours.

**8.** Rinse all the pillowcases individually until the water runs clear and then wash them with hot water and PTD (see page 24) in separate loads so they do not contaminate each other. Machine-dry and, with an iron on the linen setting, press out as many wrinkles as possible.

**9.** To make the stencil, place a piece of stencil film or Mylar over the template(s) of your choice (on page 157), and trace over it with a fine-tipped permanent marker. Place the stencil film on a self-healing cutting mat and cut away the circles by placing the screw punch down flat onto the surface of the stencil film and tapping lightly with a hammer **(C)**. Leave a border of at least 1" (2.5 cm)—more, if possible—of stencil film on all sides; this will keep the bleach from breaching the side of stencil and causing unwanted marks. Take care to make sure each hole punches out cleanly and that the lines of the stencil are even. You may want to do a few practice punches if this process is new to you.

**10.** Use the permanent marker to draw an arrow pointing upward at the corner of the stencil. This will help to orient the pattern while you are working.

**11.** After the stencil is cut, prepare the bleach paste. Cover your worktable with newsprint to protect the surface. Always work in a well-ventilated area when you are using bleach paste to avoid inhaling harmful fumes, and wear your safety mask. In a small glass container, stir together approximately 4 tablespoons (60 ml) of bleach paste thickener with 3 tablespoons (45 ml) of pure bleach and stir. The viscosity of the paste should be like thick gravy.

**12.** Starting in one corner of the pillow cover, hold the stencil firmly against the fabric and use the end of the stencil brush to pick up just a small amount of bleach paste. Use the flat surface of the stencil brush to work the bleach paste into the fabric through the holes in the stencil. If the bleach mixture is the proper ratio, the color should begin to fade right away; sometimes the initial color that is revealed can be tan, orange, or pale pink. As the bleach has more time to react with the fiber, it will continue to lighten. Note that if you have reached a very dark indigo color, you may need to add more bleach to the paste mixture to achieve the desired amount of bleaching.

**13.** Apply more bleach paste as needed to fill in the stencil. Pick up the stencil and wipe away any stray bleach paste from the back side with a paper towel. Rotate the stencil about 45 degrees as you work to give the pattern an organic feeling. Review the photograph on page 124 for ideas about how to arrange the stencil motifs **(D)**, using one or both stencils as desired.

**14.** The bleach paste can sit on the fabric for up to 3 hours before washing, but no longer—it could damage the linen fibers. Rinsing is not necessary. Machine-wash the pillow covers in hot water using a PTD and hang to dry. Iron to remove any wrinkles before placing the inserts inside.

**15.** If you have bleach paste remaining, store it covered; it will stay active for up to 24 hours.

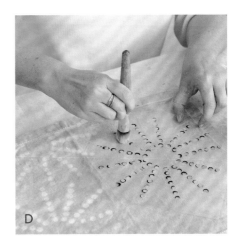

D

# Confetti Quilt

*This Confetti quilt is fun to dye, and the simple but elegant hand quilting inspired by Indian Kantha quilts makes this piece an heirloom. The color palette of cyan, yellow, and magenta dyes mix together beautifully to create little pops of green, orange, and purple where the colors blend; the bright hand-quilted stripes tie it all together. This quilt is a collaboration with Portland-based quilt artist and designer Jen Bailly (she also worked on the patchwork quilt project on page 151). Jen is fantastically talented and I am always inspired by her textile work!*

## DYER'S NOTES

This project would be lovely in another color palette as well, but remember to make sure that the colors you choose work with cold water—colors like black that require hot water will not work with this cold water application. Test your dyes carefully before working on the final project.

## SUPPLIES FOR DYEING

Dyer's Kit (see page 20), including several pairs of disposable gloves and a clean 9 × 12' (2.7 × 3.7 m) plastic or canvas drop cloth

4 yards (3.7 m) of lightweight linen, 58" (148 cm) wide
(a quilter's cotton would also work well)

Fiber-reactive dyes in cyan, yellow, and magenta (I used Procion MX in Turquoise, Bright Yellow, and Magenta)

Soda ash soak (see page 27)

Spray bottle with a fine mist setting

½ yard (18"/45 cm) of linen or cotton for testing the dye and shakers (any width is fine)

Saltshakers, one for each color of dye

Masking tape and toothpick (optional—see step 3)

Professional textile detergent (see page 23)

| LEVEL: | SKILLS LEARNED: | FIBER: | DYE: |
|---|---|---|---|
| ●●●○ | Direct dye application, color blending, working large scale, hand quilting | Cellulose (linen) | Fiber-reactive dye |

TIP

You can also use a linen piece 45 to 50" (112.5 to 125 cm) wide for this project, but note that the final dimensions of the quilt will be smaller, as the linen will also shrink a bit in the wash. Adjust the size of the batting, too (you'll need less than is listed under Supplies for Quilting on the opposite page).

## DYEING DIRECTIONS

**1.** Scour the fabric (see page 26). Cut the linen yardage into two pieces that are 58 × 72" (145 × 180 cm). Place the pieces of linen and the test fabric into the prepared soda ash soak and leave until fully saturated, at least 30 minutes.

**2.** While the linen is soaking, prepare the dye. Wear your protective mask as you add 1 tablespoon (14.5 g) of powdered dye into a saltshaker, putting only one color in each shaker **(A)**. Fill the plastic spray bottle with warm water and set the nozzle to a fine mist.

**3.** You will create the speckled dye effect by sprinkling a very fine, even coat of the dry powdered dye onto the wet linen fabric. It is a good idea to test the amount of dye that comes out of the shakers onto the test fabric. If the holes in the shakers are too large and allow too much dye to shake out for your liking, try covering them with masking tape and then poking smaller holes into the tape with a toothpick. You can always add more dye, but it is impossible to take any away! Wear your gloves and mask while you're shaking out the powdered dye.

**4.** Place a clean drop cloth on a flat surface and smooth out any wrinkles. Once the linen is soaked through, remove the test piece and try out your shakers. When you're happy with the results, remove one large piece of linen from the soda ash soak and wring out as much excess liquid as possible back into the bucket. Lay the linen flat on top of the drop cloth and smooth out any wrinkles. Starting with yellow, shake an even layer of dye over the linen, working from side to side, so that the entire cloth has a fine dusting of color. The color will develop slowly as the powdered dye dissolves into the soaked fabric. Allow the dye to dissolve and expand for 10 to 15 minutes before adding more yellow or moving on to another color. If your fabric dries quickly while you are working, gently spray a fine mist of water onto the cloth until it is damp again and the dye begins to dissolve. Add more yellow to fill in any empty spots as needed.

**5.** Repeat the process with magenta dye **(B)**, followed by the cyan dye **(C)**. Mist the fabric as necessary in between colors.

**6.** Thoroughly clean the drop cloth (or flip it over to its clean side) before repeating steps 4 and 5 on the second length of linen. A word of caution: any stray powdered dye will transfer to the clean fabric and may cause unwanted spots of color, so take care that your work surface is clean.

**7.** Allow the fabric to dry completely before moving it. When dry, gently fold the linen and wash in the machine on the cold setting with PTD (see page 24). Machine-wash once more in hot water with PTD and then machine-dry.

**8.** With your iron on the linen setting, steam both pieces until flat.


## SUPPLIES FOR QUILTING

2 dyed pieces of linen

1 package of twin-size batting (72 × 90" [180 × 225 cm])

Roll of painter's tape

Water-soluble marking pen (do not use an air-dry pen)

Curved safety pins for basting

Size 8 perle cotton in three different colors (Jen used Wonderfil Eleganza in White, Laser Lemon, and Let's Pink)

Quilting needle (3" [7.5 cm] soft sculpture doll needles are recommended)

Thimble

1 yard (.9 m) of yellow fabric for binding, at least 45" (112.5 cm) wide

Basic sewing supplies, including sewing machine and thread in a complementary color


## QUILTING DIRECTIONS

**1.** Choose one of the dyed pieces of linen for the quilt back. Place it right-side down on a clean hard surface like the kitchen floor. Make sure the backing is flat and smooth. Starting at the center of one of the sides, use the painter's tape to secure the quilt back to the floor. Place a piece of tape about every 3" (7.5 cm), or the width of your fist, along the side. Work your way out from the center until the entire side is taped down.

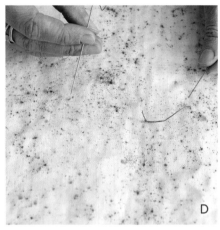

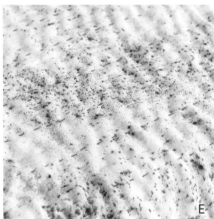

**2.** Move to the opposite side and pull taut so there is no slack in the fabric, but not so tight that the fabric is stretched. Add tape to this side, and then continue taping around the remaining sides until the entire back is taut and taped down.

**3.** Place the batting on top of the quilt back and smooth. Trim to be the same size as the backing. Trim the remaining dyed piece of fabric (for the quilt front) to 51 × 66" (127.5 × 165 cm) and center it on top of the batting and smooth. There should be about a 3" (7.5 cm) margin of backing/batting extending around all the edges, depending on shrinkage.

**4.** Using a yardstick and water-soluble marking pen, mark a vertical line down the middle of the quilt top. On either side of the first marked line, measure 1½" (4 cm) and mark the next lines. Continue until the entire quilt is marked.

**5.** Starting on any side, use the curved safety pins to pin the layers together, being sure to catch all three layers together as you go. Place pins about 3" (7.5 cm) or a fist's width apart, working your way around the quilt until the entire quilt is secured.

**6.** Pull off the tape, and it's ready to quilt. You'll be using the "big stitch" technique to quilt the layers together. To begin, cut a 36" (90 cm) piece of perle cotton and tie a small knot. Starting 2" (5 cm) from where you want the quilting to begin, insert the needle through the top and batting only, with the needle emerging on the right side of the top **(D)**. Gently tug on the knot until it pops through the quilt top and is caught in the batting.

**7.** Insert the needle through all layers to make the first stitch. Rock the needle up and down through all layers, "loading" 3 or 4 stitches on the needle. Push the needle with a thimble on your middle finger and pull the needle through.

**8.** When the thread runs out, make a small knot close to the quilt top and then take one last stitch through the top and batting only. Pull the knot through the fabric into the batting. Clip the thread near the surface of the quilt. Continue stitching until all the marked lines have been quilted **(E)**. Trim all the layers even with the quilt top.

**9.** To bind the quilt, cut 4" (10 cm) strips by the width of the yellow binding fabric. Use seven of the strips and sew each together using a ½" (1.3 cm) seam, creating a continuous binding strip. Press it in half lengthwise to create a long folded strip.

**10.** Starting about 15" (37.5 cm) away from a corner, align the raw edge of one end of the binding with the raw edge of the quilt back, right sides together.

Leave a tail of approximately 4" (10 cm) of unpinned binding at the beginning, then pin several inches (cm) of binding to the quilt, moving toward its corner.

**11.** Do a quick alignment around the rest of the quilt, without pinning, to make sure none of the seams of the quilt binding will end up at a corner of the quilt, where the seam allowances would create too much bulk. If you find a seam at a corner, change the starting point of the binding and check again.

**12.** Using a ⅝" (1.5 cm) seam allowance, start to sew the quilt binding to the side of the quilt, leaving the beginning tail free. Use pins if needed to keep the edges aligned. Stop sewing before you reach the corner of the quilt, ending the seam ⅝" (1.5 cm) from the edge. Sew a few backstitches, cut the thread, and remove the quilt from the machine.

**13.** Fold the unsewn quilt binding straight up, positioning it so that its right edge is parallel with the next side of the quilt to be bound. Coax the lower edge of the strip to form a 45-degree angle.

**14.** Fold the binding down, leaving the top of the fold flush with the edge of the quilt top and its raw edge aligned with the next side of the quilt to be bound. The 45-degree angle should be intact under the fold. (If you're new to quilting, this is called a "mitered corner." You can find lots of examples of this technique with a quick Internet search.)

**15.** Pin the quilt binding to the side of the quilt or align it as you sew. Beginning where the first seam ended, sew 2 to 4 stitches down the next side, backstitch to the beginning of that seam for security, and then continue to sew the next side.

**16.** Sew the binding to the remaining sides of the quilt, mitering each corner as in steps 12–15. End the final seam 4 to 6" (10 to 15 cm) from the original starting point and backstitch.

**17.** Trim the excess binding, leaving a tail that's long enough to overlap the first unsewn tail by about ⅝" (1.5 cm). Sew the two tails together and finish sewing the binding down.

**18.** Turn the binding toward the front of the quilt and hand stitch using a ladder stitch. See the finished binding in photo **F**.

# Indigo Upholstery Fabric

*I have always loved the lines of my grandmother's classic wingback chair. When I inherited this chair a few years ago, I wanted to give it a new life with hand-dyed upholstery in a bold indigo stripe. The contrast between the classic lines of the chair and the unexpected shibori pattern on the fabric makes a striking statement. You can use these instructions to make unique upholstery fabric to complement any style of furniture.*

## SUPPLIES

Dyer's Kit (see page 20), including a 5-gallon (19 L) bucket

7 yards (6.3 m) of upholstery-weight linen, 56" (140 cm) wide (see Fabric Notes for more information about estimating yardage for your project)

Indigo kit (see Resources, page 158) or indigo vat (see page 30)

5-gallon (19 L) container of clean water

## FABRIC NOTES

Check with your local fabric store or upholstery studio to figure the amount of yardage needed for your particular chair (or other piece of furniture). A typical wingback style like this one takes about 7 yards (6.3 m) of material 56" (140 cm) wide. Take a photo of your chair with you to the store so the professionals can help you estimate how many yards to buy. You can also do this project with a cotton upholstery fabric, but make sure to dye a test sample before buying the entire yardage. In step 1, I suggest cutting your upholstery fabric in half before dyeing to make it easier to handle— before doing this, make sure to ask your upholsterer if they can work with yardage that has been split into several cuts.

| LEVEL: | SKILLS LEARNED: | FIBER: | DYE: |
|---|---|---|---|
| ●●○○ | Tub dyeing, folding, adding resists, dyeing with indigo, working large scale | Cellulose (linen) | Indigo |

## DIRECTIONS

**1.** Seven yards (6.3 m) of upholstery-weight fabric is heavy and it is difficult to keep the fabric even during folding. To make it more manageable, cut the fabric into two lengths of 3½ yards (3.2 m) each. Scour the fabric (see page 26).

**2.** Fold one of the pieces in half lengthwise (selvedge edge to selvedge edge), so the fabric is approximately 28" (70 cm) wide, and smooth away any wrinkles. Working on a clean tabletop, begin accordion-folding the fabric, with each fold being 3 to 4" (7.5 to 10 cm) wide **( A )**—also make sure that the floor under the table is clean if the fabric is touching the floor when you are folding.

**3.** When the entire piece of fabric has been folded, secure it in place with a rubber band or two, if it is helpful. Wrap the linen with twine—tie the twine more tightly for more white in the final pattern or more loosely for more indigo blue in the finished project **( B )**. Bind the second piece as you did the first. (This is a variation of the Accordion Folding pattern on page 37.) Soak the bound pieces of linen in a bucket of clean water until the fabric is soaked through, at least 20 minutes.

## DYER'S NOTES

When clean water absorbs into a fiber, it takes up the space that would otherwise be filled with dye. In the case of indigo, this causes the pattern to become more white. If you prefer the patterns to have very little white and be mostly indigo with very little pure white space left in the pattern, skip the soaking process in step 3 and add the bound, dry linen directly to the indigo vat.

**4.** Remove one of the pieces of linen from the bucket, wring out any excess water, and place it in the indigo vat. (Leave the second piece in the bucket of water for now.) Using heavy gloves or a stir stick, press the fabric down into the vat so all the fabric is evenly covered with dye and no part of the fabric is exposed to air **( C )**; fabric exposed to the air while dyeing in the vat will oxidize and cause dark spots in the pattern. Set a timer for 45 minutes, stirring the fabric gently every 10 to 15 minutes to make sure that the bound fabric is dyeing evenly.

**5.** After 45 minutes, remove the linen from the vat and gently wring out as much indigo as possible back into the bucket. Unfold the fabric, remove the resists **(D)**, and allow it to oxidize. Be careful not to let the wet fabric fold onto itself—it will cause smudges and possibly transfer indigo to the pristine white parts of the pattern.

**6.** When the fabric has oxidized, rinse it with cold water. Wring out the excess water and machine-wash in hot water using a PTD (see page 24).

**7.** Repeat the dyeing instructions in steps 4–6 for the second piece of fabric; you can put it in the indigo vat as soon as you remove the first piece.

**8.** Machine-wash the second piece of linen on its own. Machine-dry. Discard or store the indigo vat according to the instructions on page 33.

**9.** Take the fabric to a professional upholsterer to have it placed on your chair; if you have the skills to do it yourself, go for it!

# Ribbon Top Baskets

*I love the look of hand-dyed cotton ribbon on these rustic baskets. I use baskets all over the house to rein in toys, store extra blankets, corral laundry—anything you can think of. This project is a simple way to add some extra color and pattern to a room (as well as serve a useful function). Look for baskets with coils and an open weave so a large crewel needle can fit through. I always search for good baskets at thrift stores, garage sales, and discount retailers. Since most cotton ribbons are coated in a heavy starch that resists the dye, this project uses a special form of scouring to make cotton ribbons more dye-friendly.*

## SUPPLIES

Dyer's Kit (page 20)

1 spool of 100% cotton twill tape, 1" (2.5 cm) wide (you may need more or less depending on how large your baskets are)

Large stockpot (do not use again for food preparation)

½ cup (114 g) of soda ash

Hot plate (optional)

Soda ash soak (see page 27)

Fiber-reactive dye in navy blue (I used Dharma Fiber Reactive Dye in Strong Navy)

A shallow, flat-bottomed plastic, glass, or ceramic container

Large crewel needle

Large coil basket(s) (the largest shown here is approximately 20 × 28" [50 × 70 cm])

| LEVEL: ●●○○ | SKILLS LEARNED: Scouring by simmering, dip dyeing | FIBER: Cellulose (cotton) | DYE: Fiber-reactive dye |
|---|---|---|---|

## DIRECTIONS

**1.** Unspool the twill tape and place it in a large pot with enough water to cover, ½ cup (114 g) of soda ash, and a drop of PTD. Simmer on a hot plate or the stovetop for about an hour, stirring frequently, to scour and release all the starches from the ribbon **(A)**. Do not use the stockpot for cooking after you have scoured the ribbon in it.

**2.** After the ribbon has simmered for an hour, discard the scouring water and rinse the ribbon with clean, cool water. Place the rinsed ribbon into the prepared soda ash soak for at least 15 to 20 minutes, until fully saturated.

**3.** While the ribbon is soaking, prepare the dye. Put on your safety gear; in a glass jar or small container, make a slurry (see page 19) of navy blue dye by adding 1 rounded teaspoon (4.5 g) of dye to about 1 cup (240 ml) of warm water. Mix well until all of the dye is dissolved. Pour the dye into the shallow container; it should be about ¼" (6 mm) deep **(B)**.

**4.** Wearing gloves, remove the twill tape from the soda ash soak and begin to wind it back into a spool, squeezing any excess liquid as you go.

**5.** When the ribbon is wound back into a spool, place it flat-side down in the shallow dyebath **(C)**.

**6.** Let the spool sit for at least 45 minutes in the dye. If you would like the dye to reach farther up the sides of the ribbon, slowly add more dye to the bath, little by little. Note that the dye will gradually absorb into the twill tape and wick up into the fiber, so take care to add dye slowly and wait several minutes after each addition to see how much dye absorbs into the cotton. Flip the spool over and repeat to dye the opposite edge.

## TIP

When you are looking for a container for the dye, search for one that allows the entire spool of ribbon to sit flat. This will help the ribbon dye more evenly.

**7.** Place several layers of paper towels or newsprint on your work surface. When the ribbon has reached your desired shade, remove it from the dye, and let it rest on top of the paper. The ribbon will drip excess dye, so make sure there is plenty of paper underneath and that your work surface is sufficiently protected **(D)**.

**8.** When the ribbon has set for about an hour, rinse it well in cool water with a few drops of a PTD. When the water runs clean, wring out any excess water and hang the ribbon to dry. After the ribbon is dry, iron flat.

**9.** Measure and cut a 3-yard (2.7 m) length of twill tape. Thread it through eye of a large crewel needle and tie a knot to keep the ribbon from pulling loose while you're stitching. Working from the inside of the basket, find a place to weave the needle though and pull the twill tape to the front of the basket. Continue weaving the twill tape through the coils of the basket in a simple whip stitch **(E)**.

**10.** If you run out of ribbon before reaching the end, measure and cut another length of twill tape. Tie it to the existing length of tape and tuck the knot under the woven ribbon. Continue weaving the tape around the entire top of the basket **(F)** and tie off with a knot when finished. Hide the knot under the woven ribbon, if you prefer.

## TIP

Save any leftover ribbon for wrapping gifts or sewing projects. You will be amazed at how useful (and inspiring) it is to have a few yards of beautiful twill tape around the house.

# Night Sky Curtains

*These dark and dramatic indigo-dyed te-kumo (spider web) shibori drapes are perfect for turning any room into a cozy, stylish space. While the tying and dyeing of these drapes is not particularly difficult, it is time consuming and requires some careful preparation for the best results. Anyone who enjoys crafts like hand quilting or crochet will appreciate this project. Wrapping the circles of fabric in tightly wound thread is very meditative; I suggest doing the binding in a few sittings before setting up the dyebath.*

## SUPPLIES

Dyer's Kit (see page 20), including a 5-gallon (19 L) bucket

100% cotton curtains (each panel shown here is 57 × 98" [142.5 × 245 cm])

Small plate or bowl, approximately 4" (10 cm) in diameter

Washable fabric marker

Yardstick

Heavy-duty polyester thread

Large 5-gallon (19 L) container of clean water

Indigo kit (see Resources, page 158) or indigo vat (see page 30)

| LEVEL: | SKILLS LEARNED: | FIBER: | DYE: |
|---|---|---|---|
| ●●●○ | Tub dyeing, binding, adding resists in a complex pattern, dyeing with indigo, working large scale | Cellulose (cotton) | Indigo |

A

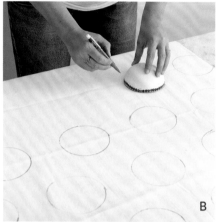

B

C

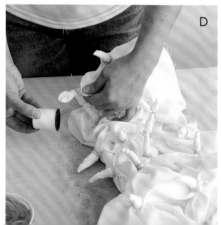

D

## DIRECTIONS

**1.** Scour the curtains (see page 26).

**2.** Lay out the first curtain on a large, clean surface and smooth it flat. If you work on the floor, I suggest placing a rolled towel under your knees to protect them.

**3.** Starting at the top left-hand corner of the curtain, about 4" (10 cm) from the finished edge, trace around the bowl with the washable fabric marker. (You can make the circles larger or smaller if you like, depending on the scale of your curtain panels.) Continue tracing circles across the width of the curtain, using a yardstick to help space them evenly; place one every 4" (10 cm) or so. Stagger the pattern for the second row of circles **(A)**. Continue, staggering the rows, until the entire curtain is covered in the hand-drawn circles **(B)**. These markings will guide you as you bind each circle with rubber bands before wrapping them tightly in thread.

**4.** Repeat steps 2 and 3 for the second curtain panel.

**5.** Secure a rubber band tightly over each circle as shown in photo **C**, continuing until the entire panel is bound. Repeat with the second curtain panel.

## TIP

For the binding, I suggest polyester thread because it will resist the dye more than cotton thread, giving cleaner lines. You could also use fishing line or dental floss in place of thread in this project, so there are several interesting options to explore.

**6.** After the rubber bands are firmly in place, begin wrapping each bound section of fabric with heavy-duty polyester thread. To do so, first secure the loose end of the thread under the rubber band to keep it in place while you wrap. Holding the spool of thread in your hand, wrap the thread as tightly as you can, leaving as little fabric uncovered as possible **(D)**. When complete, snip the thread and secure in place with another small rubber band. (This spider-web pattern is a more tightly wound variant of the Circles pattern on page 40). Continue tightly winding thread over every bound section in both curtain panels.

**7.** After the panels are fully tied, I recommend inspecting them to make sure that you have not missed any spots—it is easy to skip areas when you are working on such a big project. Soak the curtains in clean water until saturated, at least 30 to 45 minutes.

**8.** While the curtains are soaking, prepare the indigo vat according to the instructions on page 30 or in your kit. Set up your drying rack so it is ready to go when the curtains come out of the dyebath.

**9.** Remove one panel from the bucket and wring out any excess water while wearing heavy gloves. (Leave the other panel to soak for now.) Place this curtain panel in the indigo vat and hold it down until all the air bubbles are released and the curtain stays submerged under the dye. If possible, do not allow any one part to be exposed to the air while in the dye vat. This will cause that part of the cotton to oxidize and turn a darker color of indigo, potentially causing dark and uneven spots on your project. Set a timer for 45 minutes and stir and turn the curtain frequently to help it dye evenly.

**10.** After the cotton has had time to absorb the indigo and the entire piece is a bright lime green (**E**), remove the curtain from the indigo bath and wring it gently to remove excess dye, being careful not to disturb the thread and tied areas. Let the curtain oxidize on the drying rack, still tied, until the cotton is a deep indigo blue. Repeat this process several times; the more times the process is repeated, the darker the final indigo tone.

**11.** Repeat steps 9 and 10 for the second curtain panel. When each curtain has reached the desired shade, wring as much excess dye as possible back into the indigo vat and let each panel oxidize fully without removing the thread.

**12.** If possible, allow the curtains to dry slightly before removing the binding. This will keep the wet and still-active indigo from creeping into the dry, white areas of the shibori pattern. Remove the rubber bands and thread from the curtains. You can unwind the thread, or pull gently from the edges of the bound areas and the rubber bands and thread may simply roll off, making removal less tedious.

**13.** When all the thread and rubber bands have been removed (**F**), rinse the curtains with cold water until the water runs clean, or wash them on a rinse cycle with cold water before you machine-wash in hot water with a PTD (see page 24). If the machine is overloaded with indigo, it will stain the white parts of the shibori and make them a pale blue instead of crisp white. Machine-dry and iron before hanging.

E

F

# Mud Cloth Chair

*This lovely chair looks stylish indoors or out and mixes well with all sorts of hand-dyed patterns. The design for this project was inspired by mud cloth, a very beautiful black-and-white, traditional African textile rich with pattern. Garments from hand-dyed mud cloth were traditionally worn as protective clothing, keeping the wearer safe from evil spirits who were meant to be confused by the meandering geometric patterns. Each piece of mud cloth tells a story in the arrangement of the symbols, which are often passed down from mother to daughter.*

## SUPPLIES

Dyer's Kit (see page 20), including one wide 5-gallon (19 L) plastic container for dyeing and one 5-gallon (19 L) plastic container for curing

100% cotton butterfly chair in natural canvas

Soda ash soak (see page 27)

Fiber-reactive dye in black (I used two ⅔-ounce [19 g] containers of Procion MX in Jet Black)

2 gallons (7.6 L) of hottest tap water

2 gallons (7.6 L) of boiling water

4 cups (840 g) of dyer's salt

8½ × 11" (21.5 × 28 cm) piece of plastic stencil film or sheet of medium-weight Mylar (one piece or sheet for each template used)

Templates (see page 157)

Fine-tipped permanent marker

Craft knife

Self-healing cutting mat

Bleach

Bleach-thickening paste

Small stencil brush

LEVEL:
●●●○

SKILLS LEARNED:
Tub dyeing, dyeing solid colors, cutting stencils, working with bleach paste

FIBER:
Cellulose (cotton)

DYE:
Fiber-reactive dye

## TIPS FOR SUCCESSFUL STENCILING

Stenciling is a time-honored technique that can be used to create very modern, fresh designs. Here are a few tips for success:

• work on flat surface

• use a very small amount of medium (paint, dye, bleach paste, etc.)

• use the right brush—a stencil brush has a flat top

• use the right technique—the brush is meant to be used flat, held at a 90-degree angle to the surface being decorated and tapped over the stencil, not brushed across the stencil

## DIRECTIONS

**1.** Remove the chair cover from the frame and scour it (see page 26).

**2.** Soak the chair cover in the prepared soda ash soak until fully saturated, at least 1 hour.

**3.** Prepare the dyebath after the cover has finished soaking; when working with black it is best that the water be as hot as possible when the items are introduced. In the 5-gallon (19 L) container, add approximately 2 gallons (7.6 L) of the hottest tap water you can get and approximately 2 gallons (7.6 L) of boiling water. Wearing your safety gear, stir in 4 cups (840 g) of dyer's salt and add two full containers of black dye to the salt and water. Stir until all the dye has dissolved.

**4.** Wring out as much water as possible from the chair cover and add it to the container **(A)**. Using a stick or long spoon, submerge the chair cover in the hot dyebath. Take care not to burn your hands. Set a timer for 4 hours and stir and turn the chair cover frequently to help it dye more evenly.

**5.** After 4 hours, remove the chair cover from the dyebath and wring out as much of the dye as possible. Note that when you are dyeing heavy fabrics and items with structure, it can often be difficult to wring out the dye. For this reason, put the cover into a large plastic bag and set it inside of a large plastic storage container to catch any excess dye. Leave it to cure for 12 to 24 hours.

**6.** After the chair cover has cured, rinse in cold water until the water runs clear. Machine-wash on hot with a PTD (see page 24), and machine-dry.

**7.** Iron out as many wrinkles as possible from the chair cover.

**8.** To make the stencil, place a piece of stencil film or Mylar over a template on page 157 and trace over it with a fine-tipped permanent marker. Place the stencil film on a self-healing cutting mat and use a craft knife to cut away the pattern **( B )**, leaving a border on all sides if possible. This will keep the bleach from breaching the side of the stencil and causing unwanted marks.

**9.** Use the permanent marker to draw an arrow pointing up at the corner of the stencil. This will help to orient the pattern while you are working.

**10.** Repeat steps 8 and 9 for the other templates on page 157.

**11.** After the stencils are cut, prepare the bleach paste. Cover your worktable with newsprint to protect the surface. Always work in a well-ventilated area when you are using bleach paste to avoid inhaling harmful fumes, and wear your safety mask. In a small glass container, stir together approximately 4 tablespoons (60 ml) of bleach paste thickener with 3 tablespoons (45 ml) of pure bleach and stir. The viscosity of the paste should be like thick gravy **( C )**.

**12.** Starting in the upper left-hand corner of the chair cover, hold the stencil firmly against the canvas and use the end of the stencil brush to pick up just a small amount of bleach paste. Use the flat surface of the stencil brush to work the bleach paste into the canvas through the cuts in the stencil. If the bleach mixture is the proper ratio, the black should begin to fade right away. Sometimes the initial color that is revealed when the bleach is applied can be tan, orange, or pale pink, but as the bleach has more time to react with the fiber it will continue to lighten. Add more bleach paste as needed and fill in the stencil **( D )**. Pick up the stencil and wipe away any stray bleach paste from the back side with a paper towel.

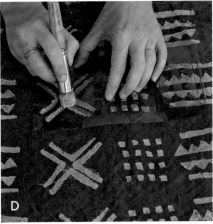

**13.** Apply bleach paste through the other stencils as in step 12 to complete the pattern. Wait until the bleached design is revealed, then print with the bleach paste again; be sure to wipe the stray bleach paste from the back side of each stencil after each print. Continue, printing from left to right, until the entire chair is covered with pattern. If you prefer, you could also print the motifs individually, rotating them every now and then for a more random design.

**14.** The bleach paste can sit on the fabric for up to 3 hours before washing, but no longer—it could damage the cotton fibers. Rinsing is not necessary. Machine-wash the chair cover in hot water using a PTD and hang to dry. Iron to remove any wrinkles before placing it back on the frame.

**15.** If you have bleach paste remaining, store it covered; it will stay active for up to 24 hours.

### DYER'S NOTES

While you can skip dyeing the chair black and simply buy a black canvas chair cover, I prefer the warm tone that the hand-dyed chair lends and the color the natural canvas turns when it reacts with the bleach. These qualities would also translate well into a smaller project with a similar fabric as a base, such as a canvas tote bag.

# Classic Patchwork Quilt

*I took my color cues for this luxurious patchwork quilt from traditional Indian textile design—I dyed the quilter's cotton in a bright and festive mix of hot pinks and corals and used one of the rich pink colors for the stamped designs. When you are making other projects, consider adding a yard (m) or two of quilter's cotton to your dyebaths and tuck them away to use later—the mix of patterns will come together to make a truly one-of-a-kind piece.*

## SUPPLIES FOR DYEING

Dyer's Kit (see page 20), including five wide 5-gallon (14 L) plastic containers and a roll of paper towels

10 yards (9 m) of white quilter's cotton, 45" (112.5 m) wide

3 yards (2.8 m) of white quilter's cotton for the quilt back, 108" (270 cm) wide (or 9 yards [8.4 m] of 45" [112.5 cm] white cotton)

Soda ash soak (see page 27)

Fiber-reactive dye in raspberry, coral, red, pink, and tan (I used Procion MX in Raspberry, Peach, and Carmine Red, and Dharma Fiber Reactive Dye in Coral Pink and Ecru)

16 gallons (61 L) of warm water

16 cups (4.5 kg) of dyer's salt

Sodium alginate

A piece of Plexiglas or a ceramic plate larger than the stamp

Hand-carved stamp

## DYER'S NOTES

To allow for shrinkage and efficient cutting for the patchwork, you will dye a little more fabric than you actually need for the quilt top. Add the leftovers to your stash for smaller projects.

| LEVEL: | SKILLS LEARNED: | FIBER: | DYE: |
|---|---|---|---|
| ● ● ● ● | Tub dyeing, dyeing solid colors, hand stamping, direct dye application, thickening a dye, working large scale, patchwork | Cellulose (cotton) | Fiber-reactive dye |

## DIRECTIONS FOR DYEING SOLID COLORS

**1.** Cut the quilter's cotton into five 2-yard (1.8 m) lengths and scour (see page 26). Do not cut the backing piece of fabric; set it aside.

**2.** Add all five of the 2-yard (1.8 m) lengths of cotton to the prepared soda ash soak and leave for at least 20 minutes, until the cotton is fully saturated. While the cotton is soaking, prepare the dyebaths. Fill four of the 5-gallon (14 L) containers with 3 gallons (11.4 L) of warm water and 3 cups (840 g) of dyers salt. Make a slurry (see page 19) with 4 rounded teaspoons (19 g) of dye and ½ cup (120 ml) of warm water for each of the raspberry, coral, red, and pink, dyes. Add one of the slurries to each container, so you will have a total of four separate dyebaths at this stage **(A)**.

**3.** Remove the cut yardage from the soda ash soak, and wring out as much of the excess liquid as possible from each piece; add one piece to each one of the dyebaths. Let the fifth piece air dry to use for stamping later. Make sure to stir each dyebath frequently to encourage even dyeing. Set a timer for 2 hours.

**4.** While the cut yardage is dyeing, take the quilt backing fabric and fold it into thirds. Accordion-fold (see page 37) the fabric, bind with large rubber bands **(B)**, and tie tightly with twine along the length of the fabric. Soak the fabric in soda ash for at least 20 minutes, and prepare the tan dyebath while it soaks.

**5.** In the remaining 5-gallon (14 L) container, add 4 gallons (15.4 L) of warm water, a slurry of 6 rounded teaspoons (28 g) of tan dye and 4 cups (1.1 kg) of dyer's salt.

**6.** Take the backing from the soda ash soak. Wring out the excess liquid and place the backing in the tan dyebath. Set a timer for 2 hours; stir and turn the piece frequently while it is dyeing to help it dye evenly.

**7.** After 2 hours the cut lengths of cotton should be ready to come out of their respective dyebaths. Wring out each piece and wrap them tightly in separate plastic bags to cure for 12 to 24 hours.

**8.** After 2 hours in the dyebath, check the cotton backing. If the color is to your liking, remove and wring out any excess dye. (You can soak this piece for up to 4 hours if a darker tone and sharper pattern is desired.) Wrap the piece tightly in a plastic bag to cure for 24 hours. For light colors such as tan, the curing time makes a big difference in the final color. I recommend allowing the cotton backing to cure for a full day before washing.

**9.** After curing, rinse out all the cotton yardage until the water runs clear. Since all the colors for the patchwork front share a pink tone, all four dyed pieces can go in the same load of laundry without bleeding into each other—

as long as they are rinsed thoroughly first. Wash in hot water with a PTD (see page 24) and machine-dry.

**10.** When the quilt backing has cured, rinse away the excess dye with cool running water. Then remove the twine and rubber bands and discard. Machine-wash the backing in hot water with a PTD and dry.

**11.** Iron out any wrinkles in the fabric before starting to sew the quilt.

## DIRECTIONS FOR STAMPING

**1.** In a glass canning jar or a plastic container that will not be used again for food, mix together ⅓ cup (80 ml) of water and 1 rounded teaspoon (4.5 g) of raspberry dye and make a smooth slurry (see page 19). Sprinkle ¼ teaspoon (1.2 g) of sodium alginate powder into the dye slurry and stir well. Keep adding sodium alginate ¼ teaspoon (1.2 g) at the time until the dye is slightly thickened. It should be the viscosity of melted butter. Stir with a spoon or chopstick until smooth.

**2.** Cover your work surface with several layers of newsprint to keep it protected. Stack three paper towels and fold the stack in half. Place the folded paper towels onto the Plexiglas sheet or ceramic plate that can fit the entire stamp within the flat area.

**3.** Slowly pour a small amount of dye onto the center of the paper towels and allow it to absorb, adding a little more each time, until the dye has fully saturated an area the size of the stamp you're going to use **(C)**.

**4.** Wearing gloves, place the stamp facedown into the dye stamp "pad" that you just made and dab it up and down on the surface of the paper towel. Use a light hand so the dye does not pool in the carved areas of the stamp, which will bleed when they touch the surface of the cotton. You may want to test the coverage of the dye on the stamp by stamping on a damp paper towel.

**5.** Press the stamp into the pad once again to load it with dye and stamp onto the top left-hand corner of yardage; press down evenly on the entire back of the stamp with the heel of your hand and lift away. Repeat this process, stamping from left to right in a row along the entire top of the fabric, leaving about 1" (2.5 cm) between impressions. If desired, you can flip the stamp 180 degrees between impressions for visual interest.

**6.** Continue stamping on the second row, staggering the prints so they fall in between those on the top row, which creates a tile pattern **(D)**; continue until the yardage is covered. Mix another batch of dye according to the instructions in step 1, and add to the stamp pad as needed.

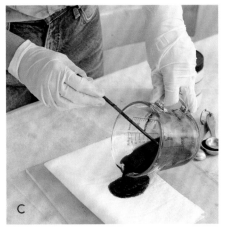

C

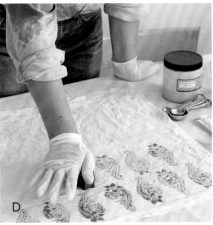

D

**7.** Allow the printed yardage to dry completely before washing. Under cold running water, rinse the printed surface of the cotton to remove any excess dye from the surface of the fabric. When the water runs clear, machine-wash with hot water and a PTD, following the manufacturer's instructions, and machine-dry. Use a hot iron with steam to smooth out wrinkles.

### TIP

To avoid picking up your stamp and printing "upside down" on your fabric, you can mark the back of your stamp with an arrow to show the correct orientation. This little trick can save you frustration later on!

## SUPPLIES FOR QUILTING

Dyed and stamped fabric (5 cut lengths + 1 large backing piece)

Basic sewing supplies, including sewing machine and thread in a complementary color

Roll of painter's tape

1 package queen-size (90 × 108" [225 × 270 cm]) batting (wool is recommended)

Curved safety pins for basting

Basic quilting tools, including a rotary cutter, square acrylic ruler, straight acrylic ruler, and self-healing cutting mat

1 yard (.9 m) of fabric in a complementary color for binding, at least 45" (112.5 cm) wide (you can also dye this to match if you prefer)

**1.** If you haven't pressed the cut lengths of fabric, do so now. From each of the five dyed/stamped lengths, cut 5 strips that are 10" (25 cm) by the width of the fabric. From each strip, cut four 10" (25 cm) squares, until you have a total of 16 blocks from each colorway, including the stamped fabric. You'll have one strip leftover in each color; choose your favorite strip and cut one more 10" (25 cm) block from that strip. In total, you will have 81 blocks to form the patchwork front of the quilt (16 in each colorway, plus 1 extra).

**2.** Arrange the squares into a pattern of your choosing, placing nine blocks in nine rows. Begin to sew the patchwork together by rows, using a ¼" (6 mm) seam allowance throughout; it's easiest to do this in two sets (one of 4 blocks and one of 5 blocks), and then stitch those units together to form one row of 9 blocks. Repeat until you have 9 rows of 9 blocks each.

**3.** Press the seams open in each row. Stitch the rows together, using pins to match the seams to one another when sewing. Once all the rows are sewn together, be sure to press all the seams open and flat.

**4.** Now you'll assemble the quilt "sandwich." (If you're new to quilting, a quick Internet search will yield lots of information about this step, along with the mitered corner technique used in steps 15 and 16.) Lay out the quilt backing flat and smooth, right-side down, on a clean hard surface such as the kitchen floor. Starting at the center of one of the sides, use the painter's tape to secure the quilt back to the floor. Place a piece of tape about every 3" (7.5 cm), or the width of your fist, to secure the side. Work your way out from the center until the entire side is taped down.

**5.** Move to the opposite side and pull taut so there is no slack in the fabric, but not so tight that the fabric is stretched. Add tape to this side and then continue taping around the remaining sides until the entire back is taut and taped down. Center the batting on top of the quilt back and smooth in place.

**6.** Center the quilt top on top of the batting and smooth. There should be a few inches (cm) of backing/batting extending around all the edges, depending on shrinkage. Starting on any side, use the curved safety pins to scoop into the quilt and grab all three layers. Pin the layers together **(E)**. Place pins about 3" (7.5 cm) or a fist's width apart, working your way around the quilt until the entire quilt sandwich is secured. Pull off the tape, and it's ready to machine quilt.

**7.** On your machine, increase the stitch length by one setting past normal; for example, if your typical stitch length is set to 2, increase to 3. Starting in the middle of the quilt next to a seam, begin quilting through all the layers in a straight line from top to the bottom of the quilt. Remove the safety pins along the way, if you'd like; if you have more advanced quilting skills, you may want to consider adding lines of quilting along each side of the seam. Repeat until all the rows have been quilted, working from the center out.

**8.** Turn the quilt 90 degrees and repeat step 7 **(F)**.

**9.** Turn the quilt on the diagonal and stitch from corner to corner of each block and then repeat from the other direction **(G)**.

**10.** To prepare for binding, square up the quilt using a large acrylic square ruler. Place it in one corner of the quilt, aligning the edges of the ruler with the edges of the quilt top. Place a long acrylic ruler above the square ruler, aligning the long edge with the quilt-top edge. Using a rotary cutter, cut away the batting and backing that extend beyond the quilt-top edge. Reposition the rulers and cutting mat as needed to trim around the entire quilt.

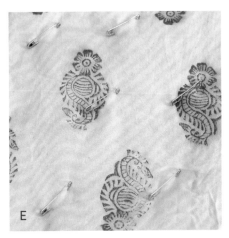

E

F

G

**11.** Cut 4" (10 cm) strips by the width of the binding fabric (you should have 9 strips in total). Sew each strip together, creating a long continuous binding strip. Then fold the strip in half lengthwise and press, creating a long folded strip.

**12.** Starting about 15" (37.5 cm) away from a corner, align the raw edge of one end of the binding with the raw edge of the quilt top, right sides together. Leave a tail of approximately 4" (10 cm) of unpinned binding at the beginning, then pin several inches (cm) of binding to the quilt, moving toward its corner.

**13.** Do a quick alignment around the rest of the quilt, without pinning, to make sure none of the seams of the quilt binding will end up at a corner of the quilt, where the seam allowances would create too much bulk. If you find a seam at a corner, change the starting point of the binding and check again.

**14.** Using a ⅝" (1.5 cm) seam allowance, start to sew the quilt binding to the side of the quilt, leaving the beginning tail free. Use pins if needed to keep the edges aligned. Stop sewing before you reach the corner of the quilt, ending the seam ⅝" (1.5 cm) from the edge. Sew a few backstitches, cut the thread, and remove the quilt from the machine.

**15.** Fold the unsewn quilt binding straight up, positioning it so that its right edge is parallel with the next side of the quilt to be bound. Coax the lower edge of the strip to form a 45-degree angle.

**16.** Fold the binding down, leaving the top of the fold flush with the edge of the quilt top and its raw edge aligned with the next side of the quilt to be bound. The 45-degree angle should be intact under the fold. This is called a "mitered corner."

**17.** Pin the quilt binding to the side of the quilt or align it as you sew. Beginning where the first seam ended, sew 2 to 4 stitches down the next side, backstitch to the beginning of that seam for security and then continue to sew the next side.

**18.** Sew the binding to the remaining sides of the quilt, mitering each corner as in steps 14–17. End the final seam 4 to 6" (10 to 15 cm) from the original starting point and backstitch.

**19.** Trim the excess binding, leaving a tail that's long enough to overlap the first unsewn tail by about ⅝" (1.5 cm). Sew the two tails together and finish sewing the binding down.

**20.** Turn the binding toward the back of the quilt and hand stitch using a ladder stitch. See the finished binding in **(H)**.

# Stencils

The stencil templates shown here are for the Points of Light Pillows (page 123) and the Mud Cloth Chair (page 147). Copy the templates and enlarge by 200% before using.

# Resources

## AMAZON

amazon.com

Although I like to shop with smaller retailers whenever possible, Amazon does make it easy to find specialty items that might be hard to find at your local store. A quick search on Amazon will reveal a wide range of options for some of the specialty items in *Hand Dyed*, such as the Indigo Stripe Hammock, Sunshine Play Tent, and Mud Cloth Chair cover. When you are searching for any kind of unique item you may want to hand dye, it is helpful to use search terms that include the fiber you are looking for followed by "natural," "undyed," or "ready to dye."

## CARGO, PORTLAND, OREGON

cargoinc.com

Cargo is an incredible store with products from around the world and a must-visit if you come to Portland. But if you live far away, Cargo has a wonderful website that is updated often; there you can find hand-carved wooden and sometimes copper stamps from India. Cargo has an amazing selection of tools from around the world, as well as hand-dyed housewares to serve as inspiration or to pair with your own hand-dyed work.

## DHARMA TRADING

dharmatrading.com

Dharma Trading has everything that you need when you first start dyeing by hand. They carry a full range of beautiful dyes and indigo for use on all fibers, as well as an incredible collection of ready-to-dye clothing and housewares, along with ribbon and fabric by the yard or bolt. The Dharma Trading staff is always available to answer questions and have helped me problem-solve many times. If you plan to purchase supplies online, Dharma Trading is a good place to start.

## IKEA

ikea.com

IKEA carries a huge variety of natural-fiber household items in white or natural undyed linen, which are ideal for hand dyeing—and they usually have fantastic prices. All IKEA products have large tags that list the fiber content, making it easy to pick the right dye for your fiber. They also carry very inexpensive, and often beautiful, fabrics by the yard.

## JACQUARD PRODUCTS

jacquardproducts.com

Products for hand dyeing from Jacquard are widely found in art and craft stores. Jacquard's Procion MX fiber-reactive dyes are bright and brilliant, and layer beautifully. Jacquard makes a number great kits for dyeing that are very simple to set up, so you can try out the techniques before you invest in a lot of supplies. I especially love the Indigo Tie Dye Kit. It is my go-to kit for dyeing with pre-reduced indigo when I am teaching. You can also buy Jacquard Products in bulk online, and they have a very helpful staff that is happy to answer your questions.

## LOCAL ART, CRAFT, AND FABRIC STORES

Most well-stocked art and craft stores will have fiber-reactive dyes and related chemicals such as soda ash, tie-dye kits, and, more often than not, indigo kits. Fabric stores are often happy to give you a small sample of a textile or let you purchase a very small amount of yardage if you are unsure about how a textile will dye.

# Acknowledgments

To my family—**Victor, Angelina, and Iris**—thank you for your steadfast support, for always encouraging my work, and for loving me unconditionally.

To my mother, **Kacey**, thank you for always supporting me from the minute I was born. Watching you be an artist and a mother showed me it was possible.

To **Dane Tashima**, I never could have imagined that our career paths and our incredible friendship would lead us to making this book together. Thank you for lending your talent, energy, and inspiration to every single image in this book.

To **Pam Morris**, your ability to create beautiful pictures knows no bounds. I learned so much watching you work.

To **Jane Gaspar**, thank you for keeping everything organized behind the scenes. It was such a pleasure getting to know you.

To **Annabelle Klachefsky**, thank you for being my brain some days and my hands others. Your help made it possible for me to keep my business running smoothly while working on this project, and for that I will be forever thankful.

To **Sarah Knight**, thank you for being my sister, my Spice. And for taking me on our trip before I started working on *Hand Dyed*. The conversation, the colors, and the ocean gave me inspiration and clarity that carried me through the whole project.

To **Jessica Donnell**, thank you for letting us bring your most precious possessions all over Oregon and for opening your incredible home to our photography. Your spaces and spirit inspired our entire crew.

To **Jennifer Bailly**, thank you so much for your beautiful quilting. From the beginning, I wanted to include quilting projects, and your incredible talent and generosity made it possible.

To **Colleen Purdy**, thank you for your help with the templates. You are a truly loyal friend and such a joy to work with.

To **Cristina Garces, Shawna Mullen, Meredith Clark**—my editors—and to **Deb Wood**, my design director: thank you all! Your encouragement and enthusiasm for my work made me trust my vision. What a gift.

To **Valerie Shrader**, my technical editor. Thank you for translating my writing and teaching style into an accurate technical document! You were always so patient and enjoyable to work with.

To **Brooke Reynolds**, who designed this beautiful book. Your ability to take my ideas and elevate them never ceases to amaze. Your artistry brings it all together. Thank you.

To **Dharma Trading Company**, thank you for so much for donating dye and all manner of supplies; I am so thankful for your incredible generosity.

To **Asher Katz** and **Jacquard Products**, I never intended to fall in love with dyeing and your gift of an indigo kit and a fiber-reactive starter kit sparked a new chapter in my life as an artist.

To **811 E. Burnside Building women**, I feel blessed to be surrounded by such powerful artists while I am in my studio. The unwavering support of this community keeps me going.

To **Joe and Karen Goodrich** and **Lainie and Randal Koch**, thank you so much for letting us photograph in the Meadow. Your beautiful homes and gardens have always given me something to aspire to.

To **Arica, Josh, Gus**, and **Nora Venti**, thank you for hosting our little book team and feeding us the most loving and delicious meals.

To all the shops and makers here in Portland, Oregon, that loaned us treasures: **Solabee Flowers & Botanicals, Cargo, Pigeon Toe Ceramics, Palace, Tiro Tiro, Rejuvenation, Boet**, and **Seven Sisters**—thank you, ladies. Your support means so much to me.

And to the readers of *Hand Dyed*. I made this for you. Thank you for choosing me as one of your teachers.

**ANNA JOYCE** is an artist and textile designer best known for her vibrant hand-dyed clothing and housewares collections. Anna draws deep inspiration from the colors in nature, and her hand-dyed pieces are sold around the world. Anna's first book, *Stamp Stencil Paint: Making Extraordinary Patterned Projects by Hand*, is a guide to hand-printing and hand-painting patterns. She lives in Portland, Oregon, with her family.

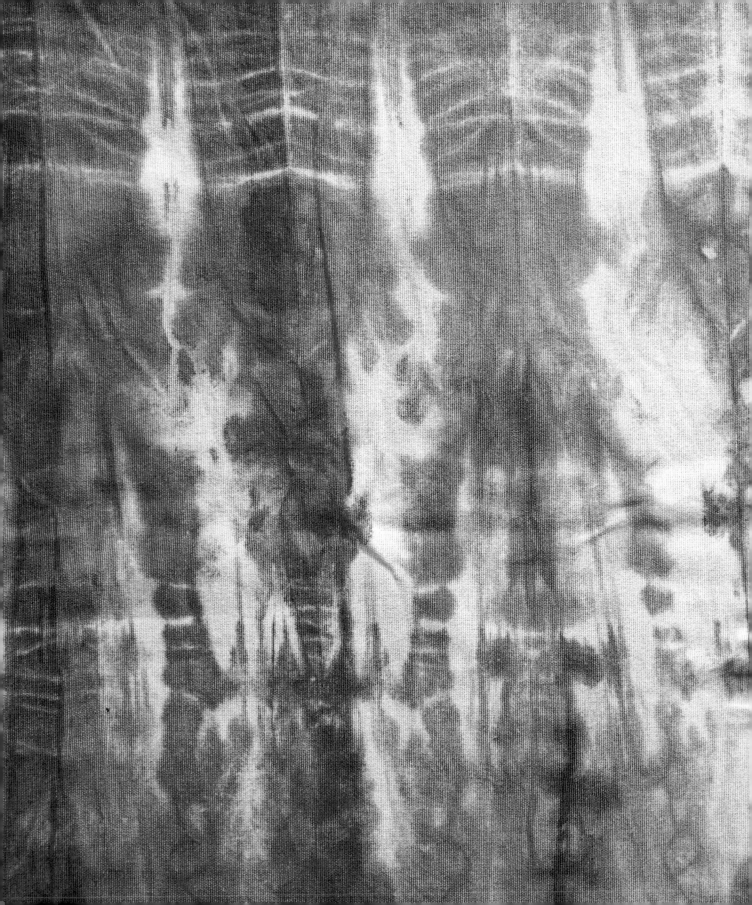